Decoded

This book is part of the Peter Lang Humanities list.
Every volume is peer reviewed and meets
the highest quality standards for content and production.

PETER LANG
New York • Bern • Berlin
Brussels • Vienna • Oxford • Warsaw

Decoded

New Essays on Zadie Smith

Edited by Tracey L. Walters

PETER LANG
New York • Bern • Berlin
Brussels • Vienna • Oxford • Warsaw

Library of Congress Cataloging-in-Publication Control Number: 2021035863

Bibliographic information published by **Die Deutsche Nationalbibliothek**.
Die Deutsche Nationalbibliothek lists this publication in the "Deutsche Nationalbibliografie"; detailed bibliographic data are available on the Internet at http://dnb.d-nb.de/.

ISBN 978-1-4331-6562-7 (hardcover)
ISBN 978-1-4331-6564-1 (paperback)
ISBN 978-1-4331-6486-6 (ebook pdf)
ISBN 978-1-4331-6487-3 (epub)
DOI 10.3726/b19128

80 Broad Street, 5th floor, New York, NY 10004
www.peterlang.com

Table of Contents

Introduction

Zadie Smith: Critical Essays (2008) was a groundbreaking exploration of the novels *White Teeth* (2000), *The Autograph Man* (2002), *On Beauty* (2005), and the short story "Hanwell in Hell" (2005). At the time of its publication, it made an important contribution to an emerging body of scholarship on Zadie Smith's fiction. In 2013, Phillip Tew published *Reading Zadie Smith: The First Decade and Beyond*, an indepth edited collection of essays examining Smith's writing from 2000 to 2012. Almost a decade later, Smith has authored a new novel, a book of short stories, a novella, and two collections of essays, enough fiction and non-fiction to warrant this new study. The five articles in *Decoded: New Essays on Zadie Smith*, focus on Smith's most current literary output, and examine her evolution from an optimistic champion of multiculturalism to a subdued austere realist. Once the face and voice of multiculturalism, Smith has morphed into a transnational writer who has broadened her social critique from the local to the global arena.

It's been twenty years since Smith published *White Teeth*, the novel that made her the darling of the literary establishment. *White Teeth* is by far her most successful novel. *White Teeth* sold more than 42,000 copies in its first print run and in 2002 it was adapted into a television mini-series. Subsequent novels also received critical acclaim. *On Beauty* (2005) was short-listed for the Man Booker Prize, *Swing Time* (2016) was long-listed for the Man Booker Prize, and the collection of literary criticism, *Feel Free* (2018) was awarded the National Book Critics Circle Award. Undoubtedly, Smith has affirmed her place within British arts and letters as one of the most influential contemporary British writers, comparable to esteemed British authors Salman Rushdie, Martin Amis, David Foster Wallace, and more recently, Andrea Levy and Bernadine Evaristo. When Smith published *White Teeth*, she was merely a college student with wisdom beyond her years, using her writing to wrestle with provocative issues of the day, such as religious fundamentalism, eugenics, multiculturalism, and race and identity. Today, although Smith is a mature woman (a wife and mother of two children and professor in the Creative Writing Program at New York University), there are still traces of the self-conscious teen trying to understand life's biggest questions. Since the mid aughts, Smith has been preoccupied with digital technology. Like many writers in the digital age, Smith has reconciled with technology's impact on society. Similar to the writers of the industrial age, she has been forced to adapt to a changing world, and her fiction and non-fiction reflect upon Big Tech's impact on her fiction, her craft, and the broader society. In interviews, she expresses her aversion to social media, because of its effect on her mental health, productivity, and personal relationships. As a writer who focuses on the importance of human relationships, technology is an ever present adversary and with great frequency, Smith bemoans digital technology's invasiveness and interruption of the natural world and the disconnection between the real and the manufactured worlds of the internet.

Situated squarely in her middle period, Smith continues to be a writer unafraid of pushing herself to create unique ways of crafting her stories. In *NW* and *Swing Time*, for example, polyphonic techniques are used throughout the novels. The short stories in *Grand Union* show her dabbling in different genres: dystopian fiction, surrealism, and science fiction. Smith's freedom to explore different writing styles and techniques is mostly the result of not catering to the demands of her publisher or her readership. In each of Smith's novels, novellas, and short stories, the plotlines differ and the characters are original, but the main themes: mortality, identity, empathy, and truth remain constant.

Over the years, literary critics have rarely come to a consensus about Smith writing. They are either extremely praiseworthy of her complicated plotlines, colorful characters, and comedic bent, or scathingly critical of her dense, rambling prose. This mode of writing drew the ire of author and critic James Wood, who infamously accused Smith of being a 'hysterical realist' and chided her for overloading *White Teeth* with copious amounts of detail. In an interview with Isaac Chotiner, Smith spoke with pride about writing *White Teeth*. "Whether it was good or bad or whatever, I was a kid. . ..When I look back, it feels like a lifetime, and I just can't imagine how it was written, but I'm glad of it" (Chotiner 2016). Smith's criticism of her early work has softened. Previously, she referred to *White Teeth* as being a "fat and messy" novel. As a literary critic, Smith has the ability to be both critic and subject, and on occasion she responds to her critics' opinions of her writing.

In the article, "This is How It Feels To Me," she responded to Wood's critique of *White Teeth*, as well as other writers he chastised for writing hysterical realistic prose: "The critic James Wood appeared in this paper last Saturday aiming a hefty, well-timed kick at what he called "hysterical realism". It is a painfully accurate term for the sort of overblown, manic prose to be found in novels like my own novel *White Teeth* and a few others he was sweet enough to mention" (Smith 2001). To some degree Smith agreed with Wood's assessment of her writing, but rejected grouping together the work of a novice writer like herself, with established authors and label them all as hysterical realists. Smith argued,

[A]ny collective term for a supposed literary movement is always too large a net,

> catching significant dolphins among so much cannibal tuna. You cannot place first time novelists with literary giants, New York hipsters with Kilburn losers and some of the writers that got caught up with me are undeserving of the criticism....[W]riters do not write what they want. They write what they can. When I was 21, I wanted to write like Kafka. But unfortunately for me, I wrote like a script editor for *The Simpsons* who had briefly joined a religious cult and then discovered Foucault. Such is life. (Smith 2001)

Smith readily admits to her immaturity, but at the same time criticizes Wood for generalizing and falsely categorizing some of the most relevant British authors of the day.

Wood's assessment of *White Teeth* was rejected by literary critic Heather Houser who actually praised Smith for her heavily descriptive prose, which is in alignment "with the age of information and the evolution of a new close, computational, and new materialist reader" (Houser 2020, 18). Houser explained, "For a close reader like Wood, excess description removes readers from the matter – even the mattering – of fiction; it sacrifices life in favor of glut, conceived here as a relentless gush of information. For the computational reader, such data is a reminder that literary devices are *data* that can be abstracted, aggregated, and analyzed as such" (2020, 18). These days, Smith is definitely more disciplined. Her cavalcade of ancillary characters are reworked into short stories where they can be fleshed out in greater detail. The tone of her novels has also evolved. The wittiness in *White Teeth* and *The Autograph Man* has been replaced with a darker more somber tone and moral stance, as seen in *Swing Time*.

While the tone of Smith's work is unfamiliar, the setting is classic Smith (although in *Swing Time*, *The Embassy of Cambodia*, and *Grand Union* Smith branches out geographically to the U.S. and various locations in Africa). Smith's birthplace of Willesden, North West London serves as the backdrop for five of her six novels. Over the years, Smith's depiction of Willesden has transformed. In *White Teet*h, Willesden was portrayed as a shining example of multiculturalism at work, a place where immigrants, the working class, and native Britons cohabitated peacefully. Later works, especially *NW*, *Swing Time*, and the essays in *Feel Free: Essays*, offer a less optimistic view of

Willesden and Britain in general. In "Optimism and Despair," Smith admits, "It's true enough that my novels were once sunnier places and now the clouds have rolled in. Part of this I chalk up simply to the experience of middle age. . . ." (Smith 2018c, 37). James Walton wondered whether the "calmer" and "more measured" tone of *Swing Time* and *NW* strips the narratives of the humor and uninhibitedness which made Smith's earlier novels so entertaining. Walton questioned if the seriousness has caused something to be lacking and "lost along the way?" (Walton 2016). Again drawing on Wood's criticism of Smith, Walton notes, "Wood, who felt *White Teeth* lacked "moral seriousness"- couldn't make the same claim for her later fiction" (Walton 2016). While Smith may have lost her comedic edge, her transformation from a satirical writer who wrote books to entertain her readers, to a more serious author who explores philosophical questions about morality and ethics, demonstrates her growth as an artist. Chapter two of this volume elucidates this point. James Arnett's essay on George Eliot's influence on Smith's adoption of austere realism explores the didactic qualities of Smith's later works.

A middle-aged Zadie Smith has been forced to reconcile with the severity of the times: the rise of populism in America and Europe, austerity measures, the Brexit referendum, racial uprisings, and a global pandemic. In "Fences: A Brexit Diary," Smith tries maintaining objectivity as she ruminates on the grievance politics of the white working classes and self-righteousness of middle-class liberals. Smith condemns the architects of Brexit, current and former Prime Ministers Boris Johnson and David Cameron, and politician Nigel Farage, for crafting and promoting a geopolitical capitalist agenda that stoked the flames of xenophobia and anti-immigrant fervor. She surmises, "One useful consequence of Brexit is to finally and openly reveal a deep fracture in British society that has been thirty years in the making" (Smith 2018d, 35). Even still she insists, "the world of my childhood has not yet completely disappeared" (Smith 2018d, 29). Smith might be unwilling to accept the melting pot of her childhood was a failed experiment, but she has no choice but to acknowledge how gentrification threatens the socioeconomic and racial diversity of her beloved hometown. Furthermore, she's even forced to reconcile with her own class privilege and the divisions created by socioeconomic differences which leads to the breakdown of communication and missed opportunities for meaningful interactions. The essay "Northwest London Blues" pays a nostalgic homage to Willesden. After spending many years in America, Smith is now an outsider. Nevertheless, she is still invested in local politics. Smith is disheartened by the ongoing gentrification in Willesden resulting in the destruction of her favorite bookshop and library and the construction of luxury condos brokered in private deals by local politicians who betray the public's trust. The essay is as much about local politics as it is about a "global reality in which states deregulate to privatize again and re-regulate to nationalize loss. . ..The charming fairy tale of benign state intervention...is now relegated to the land of fairy tales. . .." (Smith 2018a, 9).

Willesden remains a fixture in Smith's fiction because it allows her to write about ordinary men and women, community organizers, mail men, and domestic workers from humble beginnings, such as college students, Monica and Darryl from the short story "Sentimental Education," Fatou the domestic worker in "The Embassy of Cambodia," and troubled drug addict Nathan Bogle who is featured in *NW.* In the tradition of black British novelists Courttia Newland, Diran Adebayo, and Alex Wheatle, who have written extensively about misunderstood, ignored, working class black youth of Britain's inner cities, Smith spotlights the despair of the young black and brown men who are lost to the streets, primed to become drug dealers and addicts. Rather than pathologizing the Nathan's of the world, Smith is committed to humanizing them and (in the vein of Eliot) sharing their perspectives. Reflecting on these men, especially after the 2011 London riots, Smith expresses her impatience with politicians and the media who took the liberty of speaking on behalf of a community they treated as invisible:

> So many people are so willing to stand up and describe or comment or explain the behavior of young black men. People who have never met a young black man unless it was to cross the street to avoid him. I found all that commentary so tiring, this assumption of understanding. In Nathan's case, I wanted to leave him alone. I wanted him to speak with his own voice, as much as that is possible in fiction, and just to exist outside of commentary or control. (Smith, NPR 2012)

As a mother to a son of mixed-raced heritage, and sister to two younger brothers who have been subject to police surveillance and unjustified arrest, giving black men license to speak is personal for Smith.

Representing the culture and the language of Willesden and permitting the residents of Willesden to speak with their own voices is one of Smith's most notable strengths as a writer. Writing about Willesden allows Smith to celebrate the folk, in the same way her literary idol Zora Neale Hurston used black dialect to give voice to African Americans in rural towns. Smith has been able to capture the authentic voices of her Willesden folk. These characters hail from a diversity of perspectives, races, religions, and national identities each with their own distinct vernacular – ranging from Cockney, and the Queen's English – to Jamaican Patois, French, and (less convincingly) southern slang. Smith has perfected the art of interweaving polyphonic narratives from the subjectivities of this catalogue of characters who spring to life from her vivid imagination. Philip Tew surmises, "Smith's technique of overlaying and multiplying view-points, often refracted by others, is highly effective, adding depth to her perspectives" (Tew 2009, 102). In some of her earlier work, Smith crammed many of these characters into a single novel. *White Teeth* for example, included over thirty-five characters. Conversely, the short stories in *Grand Union*, as well as the novellas "Martha Martha," and the "Embassy of Cambodia," evidence her discipline and ability to reduce narratives to one or two subjects, resulting in clear and concise prose. These characters who stay with us long after the novels are finished, are the active players in Smith's prescient meditations on politics, religion, and culture. *Grand Union* is Smith's first compilation of short fiction – many of the stories were previously published in *The Atlantic*, *Granta*, and the *Paris Review*. The stories feature the same kinds of afflicted characters first introduced in *White Teeth* and The *Autograph Man*. *Grand Union* portrays memorable characters such as Ms. Adele, the insecure drag queen trying to come to terms with her aging body, the daily assault of racism and homophobia, and the rapid transformation of a gentrifying New York City. Kelso Cochrane is another important character. Smith draws from black British history to reimagine the life of this ambitious Caribbean immigrant from the Windrush generation whose hopes of reading law are snuffed out by the white supremacist hoodlums who kill him for sport. Critics gave mixed reviews of the collection. Johanna Thomas-Corr determined the collection lacked cohesion: "The inconsistency of quality is a serious flaw. At least eight of the 19 stories in G*rand Union* aren't very good. Two dystopian efforts…are cute ideas on the page, but dawdle along.…The best stories here are those that act as commentary on her fluctuations and doubts, that blend her criticism with the energy and verve of her fiction" (Thomas-Corr 2019). Joan Gaylord's review for the *Christian Science Monitor* was more generous than Corr's. Gaylord called the collection "a superb mélange of short stories." (Gaylord 2020). Gaylord opined,

> It goes without saying, that not every story will appeal to every reader.…This being said, when a reader finds the stories that resonate––that seem familiar because they capture aspects of contemporary life, or express an experience that reveals that people have more in common than it sometimes seems––Smith's stories seem golden. (Gaylord 2020)

Regardless of the critics' lukewarm reception, the collection was considered strong enough to be short-listed for the prestigious Rathbones Folio Prize.

With *Grand Unio*n and *Swing Time*, Smith pushes beyond her comfort zone and writes from the first-person. By her own admission, writing in first-person was always intimidating, "laborious and stressful" (Smith 2018e, 467) and she reserved the exercise mostly for essays. Once she moved to

America, she felt more confident writing from the "I" perspective, perhaps because the ethos of individualism is at the heart of the American value system. In almost every work, semi-autobiographical traces of Smith's life seep their way into the narrative. Whether it's her characterization of awkward teen-age freckled-faced biracial girls searching for identity: Irie, Zora, Tracey, or her love for black and white movies and obsession with an exhaustive list of pop-cultural icons (Fred Astaire, Katherine Hepburn, Gene Kelly, Michael Jackson and Jay Z), Smith writes *a version* of herself into her fiction. In interviews, Smith is hesitant to admit to the autobiographical qualities of her work, but given all that is known about her personal life, it is not difficult for scholars to deduce which aspects of life she draws from when creating her narratives. Like many writers, what Smith produces in her fiction is an amalgamation of snippets from her own life, intensive research, the histories of other people, and the concoctions of her vivid imagination.

Along with writing in first-person, Smith also turned her attention to female protagonists. *NW, Swing Time,* and *Grand Union* indicate an effort to focus on developing more women protagonists, specifically black women. In fact, in numerous interviews, she states she wrote *Swing Time* specifically for black girls. Early in her career she developed white male protagonists, tragic figures dealing with an existential crisis brought on by their own failure to determine their relevance or contribution to society and their families. In *White Teeth* the tragic figure is Archie Jones, the unheroic veteran who commits social and professional suicide; in *The Autograph Man* it's Alex-Li Tandem the depressed autograph collector; and finally in *On Beauty* we are treated to Howard Belsey the insecure self-destructive philandering art historian. These men are often juxtaposed against strong, independent black women such as Kiki Belsey in *On Beauty* and the unnamed mother in *Swing Time*, black women who trade domesticity for intellectual pursuits. Smith's women are unwilling to allow themselves to wallow in the disappointment and the harshness of life. Even those who go through life abused and exploited in quiet suffering, like Fatou the protagonist from *The Embassy of Cambodia*, do so with dignity and an inner strength that seems to be lacking in the male characters.

In *NW* and *Swing Time*, Smith explores the complexity of female friendships, the joys and pains of the close bonds between women built on secrets and lies, trust and loyalty. She shows how these friendships can last a lifetime, or due to jealousy and betrayal, dissolve as quickly as they began. Lifelong friendships in *NW* and *Swing Time* are strained by different ambitions, class, and envy. Ultimately, Smith reveals how friendships mold us and push us to be our best and worst selves. Smith's interrogation of the complexity of relationships stands at the heart of many of her novels, they are often riddled with conflicts fueled by the characters' failure to communicate and connect. Smith writes about failing marriages and fleeting romances, but time and again she comes back to volatile relationships between parents and children. Familial relationships are often antagonistic, brought on by power struggles between parents and children. Similar to other women writers, Smith crafts stories about strained relationships between mothers and daughters, but especially noteworthy is her treatment of fathers and their adult sons. *NW*, for example, features an intimate encounter between an aging Rastafarian, Lloyd, and his son Felix. The two sit together rifling through a book of photography capturing Lloyd's younger days as a black revolutionary fighting for the liberation of the black community. In this private moment, the two men establish their closeness. A similar scene plays out in *On Beauty* when Harold goes to visit his ailing father: "Harold looked up at Howard, the older man was already crying. His hands shook with emotion. He struggled to get up from his chair and, when he did, embraced his son delicately around his middle, for Howard towered above him, now more than ever" (Smith 2005a, 294). Smith has a soft spot for fathers, perhaps because of the close relationship with her own father, which she captures in *White Teeth*, *Swing Time*, *Changing My Mind*, and *Feel Free.*

Another common thread linking Smith's novels is the question of identity, often rooted in religion, nationality, and ethnicity. Smith shows difficulties adults and their children face as they struggle with their isolation from British society. In *On Beauty*, racialized and gendered identity politics are problematic for mother and daughter, Kiki and Zora, who feel alienated, invisible in society because of their race, gender, and their voluptuous bodies, which stand outside the margins of white society's definition of beauty. Zora relies on her intellect and devotion to an Self-Improvement Programme: of diet and exercise to gain acceptance, but as discussed in chapter five by Tracey Walters, Kiki has more difficulty. As one of few black women in her community, she feels invisible in her upscale college community.

In *Swing Time* (perhaps drawing from her own experience traveling to different parts of Africa), the protagonist has to confront her identity as a mixed-race woman in Africa, who is defined by the locals as a white woman who dances like a black woman. In *Swing Time*, geography, ethnicity, and culture complicate notions of racial classification. Smith studies race through the history of dance. In chapter four, Alberto Fernández Carbajal examines how Smith has to come to terms with the racist antics of childhood hero Fred Astaire, who not only appropriated black tap dance, but danced in blackface and marginalized tap dancers such as Jeni Legion who were instrumental in developing the artform.

Over the years, Smith has established herself as a solid essayist and public intellectual. As mentioned previously, evidence of her valued contribution to literary criticism was validated when *Feel Free* won the National Book Critics Circle Award for Criticism. Smith's essays document cultural shifts and carry us through the decades with the same irony and candor as James Baldwin or Joan Didion. Criticism is important to Smith's middle period because we see more clearly how she works through issues and how they become part of her novels. While the novel was the primary canvas for Smith to delve into heady topics, increasingly, she has turned to criticism. Non-fiction grants Smith the space to write about a variety of issues. She explained to Isaac Chotiner her motivation for writing criticism is instigated by her own curiosity, not the art of persuasion: "I still think of criticism as a beautiful and intelligent way of describing the lay of the land. When I write criticism now, I do tend to write about things I love just because I'm more motivated by that" (Chotiner 2016). Following the success of *Changing My Mind,* the essays in *Feel Free: Essays,* many previously published in *The New Yorker* and *The Guardian,* are a combination of literary and cultural criticism. By a coincidence, *Feel Free* shares the same title as her husband's (Nick Laird) collection of poetry also published in 2018. Smith is amongst a handful of contemporary writers who write fiction and nonfiction. Teju Cole, Chimamanda Adichie Ngozi, Ta-Nehisi Coates, and Namwali Serpell have all mastered the art of doing both very well.

Smith often claims to be an unqualified cultural critic, weighing in on contemporary matters just like the average person. In *Feel Free* she meditates upon major political events of the moment on both sides of the Atlantic: the historic election of Barack Obama, the first black president of the United States of America, and the controversial Brexit referendum. As a British citizen and American permanent resident, she cares deeply about what is happening politically in both nations. *Feel Free* is like *On Beauty* in essay form. In the book, arguments on left and right wing political ideology, immigration, race and racism, and class warfare, are all open for debate. Many of the topics she writes about in the essays are fleshed out in the novels and short stories (and vice versa). Imagery from *The Embassy of Cambodia*, for example, the description of a discarded statue of liberty costume and the crumpled identification card of a migrant worker, is also referenced in the essay "Love in the Gardens." The topic of fame, first discussed in *The Autograph Man*, reoccurs in "Meet Justin Bieber," and again in *Swing Time.*

Smith's essays have led to entanglements in national debates about 'cancel culture.' In "Getting in and Getting Out: Who Owns Black Pain," first printed in *Harper's Magazine* in July 2017, Smith commented on the controversy involving the public outcry against Dana Schutz's painting *Open Casket*, exhibited at the Whitney Biennial in 2016. *Open Casket* depicts the image of Emmett Till, a young African American teenager who was lynched in 1955 by a white mob for whistling at a white storekeeper. Schutz, who is white, was accused of exploiting black trauma for entertainment and profit. The artist and activist Parker Bright staged a protest against the painting and the artist and writer Hannah Black wrote an open letter (supported by a number of other artists) to the curators of the Whitney Biennial, demanding the removal and destruction of the image due to the commercialization and exploitation of black trauma. Social media was rife with opinions and Smith weighed-in. Troubled by the argument Schutz was guilty of cultural appropriation, and as a non-black person she was unqualified to paint the portrait of Till, Smith argued against the notion black suffering should only be addressed by black artists. Citing her own identity as a mixed-raced woman, along with that of her children, she rejected the respectability politics and gatekeeping of racial trauma. "When arguments of appropriation are linked to a racial essentialism no more sophisticated than antebellum miscegenation laws, well, then we head quickly into absurdity" (Smith 2018, 220). Smith's defense of Schutz was met with criticism by some on social media who suggested her mixed-raced heritage and glib attitude about the image of Till in the casket evidenced her white privilege and failure to understand the complexity and historical ramifications of cultural appropriation. In a blog, "Where Zadie Smith's Getting In and Getting Out Misses the Mark," Candace McDuffie wrote, "it's clear that she is more interested in being an ethnographer to black culture than a black woman. Although she states she is identified by herself and others as black, she centers whiteness in an essay that was supposed to focus on black pain" (McDuffie 2021). McDuffie's accusation of Smith's centering of whiteness over black pain is one also shared by Fernández Carbajal in Chapter 4.

Other essays in *Feel Free include* Smith writing about her own identity as a bi-racial English woman straddling two cultures as a mother, wife, and writer. Favorite cultural icons, Michael Jackson, Jay Z, and Joni Mitchell are also celebrated. Ever weary of technology, she unabashedly writes about her skepticism of Mark Zuckerberg and Facebook, which is discussed in Chapter 1 by Daniel South. Smith reveals her suspicions about technology's ability to colonize the minds of its users. She questions its impact on people's freedom, namely seducing consumers to become reliant on technology. The bigger danger, she contends, is to our humanity and privacy. In Smith's estimation, the novel is our last hope and a statement of resistance because a book allows one to read without the intrusion of advertisements or internet surveillance and data capturing mechanisms.

Smith is an avid reader who admits to reading more than she writes. Like most writers she receives complimentary copies of new books which enables her to keep abreast of emerging talent. She's been impressed by Yaa Gyasi, Alexandra Kleeman, Rachel Kaadzi Ghansah, Alexia Arthurs, and others. Smith is also fortunate to be surrounded by a community of writers. Her husband, who first edited her stories while the two were in college, continues to read drafts of her writing. Smith and Laird have also worked together on projects. They co-authored the children's book *Weirdo* (2021), and in an interview with Amy Jones, Smith revealed she and Laird were co-writing a screenplay, but after realizing she felt out of her element, she stepped away from the project. The American writer Dave Eggers is also a close friend. According to Smith, Eggers read an early draft of *Grand Union*. In 2020, despite her immense love for reading, it was writing that gave Smith solace at a time when the world was facing upheaval.

Intimations (2020), a slim volume of articles written during the Coronavirus pandemic, takes the form of the socio-autobiographical essay. The essays in *Intimations* are poignant meditations on the extraordinary spring and summer of 2020, a year that saw the Covid Pandemic, mass social unrest in response to structural racism and police brutality, and a contentious political landscape in both America and Britain. Smith claims the essays are not intended to be political, but she fails to adhere to her objective. In this slim collection, Smith tries making sense of life during a time of great uncertainty (royalties from the book are donated to the Equal Justice Initiative and the COVID-19 Emergency Relief Fund for New York). She explains, "What I have tried to do is organize some of the feelings and thoughts that events, so far, have provoked in me, in those scraps of time the year itself has allowed." (Smith 2020, forward). Inspired by Marcus Aurelius' *Meditations*, she was reminded: "Talking to yourself can be useful. And writing means being overheard" (Smith 2020, xii). The first few essays ruminate on mortality, purpose, and humanity, or lack thereof. Smith thinks about her life as a woman and the constraints of womanhood, fertility, and nature. She also expresses her gratitude for using her tools as a writer so she can create the world as she sees it (Smith 2020, 9). In pieces such as "Something to Do," she channels Heidegger's philosophy on fear and anxiety to address the endless days of trying to fill the hours with purposeful activities. She ponders, what is to be done with the gift of time? Writing is Smith's salvation, a vocation and a habit to fill the void. The urgency of time conjures T.S. Eliot's "The Wasteland" and Virginia Woolf's *Mrs. Dalloway,* two texts of the modernist period that also explore temporality and uncertainty. Thomas-Corr observes "Smith seems unusually anxious about time: wasting it, running out of it – or having it stolen from her. Time is freedom – to be curious" (Thomas-Corr 2019). Thomas-Corr suggests Smith "suffers from an intellectual Fomo, a rapacious interest in everything, which means just as she's trying to knuckle down and focus, she's giving herself more work" (Thomas-Corr 2019). Smith would argue she is receptive to 'more work' because it is her curiosity in all manner of things that drives her to write.

The collection also includes vignettes of neighborhood fixtures like Barbara the sexagenarian, a resilient New Yorker going about life accompanied by her cantankerous dog. Smith shows women like Barbara are unwilling or unable to join the mass exodus out of New York City for a country home, or region less hampered by the rising rates of infection and mortality. Barbra is undeterred by the panic. A steady voice of optimism, Barbara reassures Smith, they will get through this hard time. Later essays offer more direct confrontation with the ravages of COVID-19. Smith blasts an unnamed Trump administration for its (mis)handling of the pandemic. Britain's Prime Minister, Boris Johnson receives the same harsh critique. Smith spotlights how Covid has exposed the failing health system, health disparities and income inequality in America. Passionately, she uses the virus as a metaphor to address the deeply-rooted virus of racism, which devalues black life and turns a blind eye to the senseless police brutality that took George Floyd's life: "If the virus and the inequalities it creates were ever to leave us, America's extremities would fade" (80). Smith ends on a pessimistic note. She used to think there was a way forward, the end to structural racism and bigotry, but the events of the summer led her to think otherwise.

Smith has influenced a whole new generation of writers. Speculative fiction novelist, Namwali Serpell, is one such writer. The Zambian born bi-racial author began writing her 563-page intergenerational novel *The Old Drift* the same year *White Teeth* was released. The mélange of genres, histories, multiple geographic regions, and characters in *The Old Drift* are an obvious rift on *White Teeth.* By her own admission, *White Teeth* inspired *The Old Drift.* Other writers influenced by Smith are more intimately connected. In 2021, her mother, Yvonne Bailey-Smith, published *The Day I Fell Off My Island*, a semi-autobiographical bildungsroman about a Caribbean girl's migration to England and her experiences as a social worker and therapist. Bailey-Smith asserts the book was instigated by the experiences of the black immigrant mothers she counseled for many years as a psychotherapist. Bailey-Smith was adamant about writing the novel without her daughter's input. Reportedly, Zadie Smith was only permitted to see the manuscript after it was completed. Along with her mother, Smith's brother, Ben Bailey Smith, rapper, comedian, actor-turned-author, wrote *I Am Bear* (2016) a children's picture book that reportedly entered a bidding war. Next on the horizon for Zadie Smith is a novel of historical fiction, more literary criticism, and her debut play, *The Wife of Willesden*, an adaptation of "The Wife of Bath" tale from Geoffrey Chaucer's *Canterbury Tales*, premiering in the fall 2021.

Smith once said, "The first duty of a writer is to write the best book they can write. Every other duty is secondary to that one." Indeed Smith has built her career "trying to write the best book she can." She's had successes and failures, but ultimately, her curiosity and respect for her craft has made her one of the most important voices of her generation.

The five chapters that follow bring together canonized works by Smith that have received substantive critical analysis, with more recent works that are beginning to receive the same level of assessment. The first two chapters delve into Smith's philosophy about the role and responsibility of the artist, her ardent defense of the function of the novel in the digital age, and the connection between writers and readers. Chapters 3 through 5 illuminate Smith's growth as a writer, her reconceptualization of racial identity, and shifting literary techniques from hysterical realism to social realism.

In "Modelling Citizens: From a Digital to a Literary Public Sphere in *NW* and *Swing Time*," Daniel South analyzes "Generation Why" and its intervention in the perennial debate about Jürgen Habermas's concept of the public sphere. South highlights Smith's apprehension about the function of digital technology and its impact on the public sphere, specifically Smith's belief that social platforms such as Facebook are not viable sites for the recreation of the public sphere. Using novels *On Beauty*, *NW*, and *Swing Time* as examples, South argues Smith privileges the literary over the digital because unlike technology, which is data driven, it has the ability to represent the emotionality and complexity of the lived experience. Moreover, the literary allows the reader and writer to have a fair opportunity to engage in debate in accordance with the fundamental rules of rhetoric. Ultimately, he argues Smith uses her novels as "a literary model for interactions in the public sphere." James Arnett, in his chapter, "Zadie Smith's George Eliot's Spinoza and Everybody: The Ethics of Austere Realism," builds on South's discussion about Smith's views on the function of the novel and the responsibility of the writer. Drawing from the essay "*Middlemarch* and Everyone," Arnett illustrates how George Eliot's humane focused literary realism, largely influenced by Baruch Spinoza's humane philosophy, impacted Smith's shift toward austere realism. Arnett argues, Smith's appropriation of Spinoza's affective ethics and inheritance of Eliot's consciousness results in the creation of characters on the margins, those whose poverty and exploitation is often invisible, such as the exploited migrant workers in "The Embassy of Cambodia" and the "Lazy River," or despondent urban youth in *NW.* Arnett maintains, Smith believes it is the writer's duty to help readers see the plight of these individuals, so we can be more empathetic toward our fellow man and reconsider how our actions do not happen in isolation because we are all interconnected.

Matthias Stephan's chapter, "Transmodern Identity Construction in Later Zadie Smith," makes a case against Smith's use of modernism and postmodernism as adequate tools for her transcultural explorations of race and identity. Stephan suggests transmodernism offers Smith a more diversified perspective, one in which identities are not performative or fixed by the social constructs that give them meaning, nor are they limited simply to internal struggles. Stephan's analysis of "The Embassy of Cambodia," *Feel Free,* and *Swing Time*, highlights Smith's growth as a writer who has learned to reconceptualize identities from a broader perspective, understanding the local is global and the global is local. Alberto Fernández Carbajal's, "'[U]nder the Sign of Love': Blackface Minstrelsy's Trauma, Racial Exploitation, and Kinaesthetic Hauntologies in Zadie Smith's *Swing Time*," also addresses Smith's treatment of the construction of racial and cultural identities through the history of dance and the capital commodification of black culture. In his interrogation of *Swing Time*, Fernández Carbajal shows how black dance and black identity is framed through minstrelsy. Fernández Carbajal acknowledges Smith's effort to rewrite history and expose mainstream society's cultural appropriation of black dance and the blatant efforts of Hollywood to make invisible the dancers who created the intricate tap dance routines and styles attributed to revered dancers like Fred Astaire. At the same time, he accuses Smith of "tokenizing" identity. In his view, Smith's deification of Fred Astaire and other white dancers from Hollywood's Golden Age undermines the black dance legacy Smith intended to celebrate.

The final chapter, Tracey Walters's "The Quest for Knowledge: The Intellectual Woman in Zadie Smith's Novels," revisits an earlier essay by Walters on Smith's representations of black women characters in *White Teeth*, *The Autograph Man*, and *On Beauty,* which accused Smith of reducing her black women characters to denigrating stereotypes. Walters's reassessment of *On Beauty*, and analysis of "Martha Martha" and *Swing Time*, evidences numerous examples of characters who positively redefine black womanhood. She describes how these black women characters fight back against the misrecognition of their personhood by seeking out alternative postfeminist versions of womanhood mirrored from their own real and imagined communities.

Works Cited

Chotiner, Isaac. "Zadie Smith on Male Critics, Appropriation, and What Interests Her Novelistically about Trump." *Slate*, Nov 16, 2016. https://slate.com/culture/2016/11/a-conversation-with-zadie-smith-about-cultural-appropriation-male-critics-and-how-trump-interests-her-novelistically.html. Accessed August 6, 2021.

Gaylord, Joan. "Review of *Grand Union.*" *The Christian Science Monitor.* March 17, 2020. https://www.csmonitor.com/Books/Book-Reviews/2020/0317/Zadie-Smith-s-Grand-Union-is-a-superb-melange-of-short-stories. Accessed Aug 12, 2021.

Houser, Heather. "Shimmering Description and Descriptive Criticism." *New Literary History*, vol. 51, number 1 (Winter): 2020, pp. 1–22. John Hopkins University Press. DOI: https://doi.org/10.1353/nlh.2020.0000. Accessed July 17, 2021.

McDuffie, Candace. "Where Zadie Smith's Getting in and Getting Out Misses the Mark." Blog. Ploughshares. https://blog.pshares.org/zadie-smiths-getting-in-and-out/. Accessed Aug 7, 2021.

Smith, Zadie. "This Is How It Feels To Be Coloured Me." *The Guardian.* Oct 13, 2001. https://www.theguardian.com/books/2001/oct/13/fiction.afghanistan. Accessed August 12, 2021.

———. *The Autograph Man.* London: Penguin Books, 2002.

———. *Martha and Hanwell.* London: Penguin Books, 2005a.

———. *On Beauty.* London: Hamish Hamilton, 2005b.

———. *NW.* 2012. London: Penguin Books, 2012.

———. "Same Streets, Different Lives in 'NW' London." Interview by Lynn Neary, *Morning Edition*, NPR September 6, 2012. https://www.npr.org/2012/09/06/160254532/same-streets-different-lives-in-nw-london

———. *The Embassy of Cambodia.* London: Hamish Hamilton, 2013.

———. *Swing Time.* London: Penguin Books, 2016.

———. *Feel Free: Essays.* London: Penguin Books, 2018.

———. "Northwest London Blues." In *Feel Free: Essays.* London: Penguin Books, 2018a, 3–13.

———. "Generation Why." In *Feel Free: Essays.* London: Penguin Books, 2018b, 45–63.

———. "Optimism and Despair." In *Feel Free: Essays.* London: Penguin Books, 2018c, 35–41.

———. "Fences: A Brexit Diary." In *Feel Free: Essays.* London: Penguin Books, 2018d, 20–34.

———. "Life Writing." In *Feel Free: Essays.* London: Penguin Books, 2018e, 351–353.

———. "The Bathroom." In *Feel Free: Essays.* London: Penguin Books, 2018f, 354–365.

———. *Grand Union*. London: Penguin Books, 2019.

———. *Intimations*. London: Penguin Books, 2020.

———. “Something to do.” In *Intimations*, 19–28. London. Penguin Books, 2020a, 19–28.

Tew, Philip. *Zadie Smith*. Palgrave New British Fiction. New York: Palgrave, 2010.

———. *Reading Zadie Smith: The First Decade and Beyond*. Ashland: Bloomsbury Books, 2014.

Thomas-Corr, Johanna. “The Observer Zadie Smith.” *The Guardian*. Oct 14, 2019. https://www.theguardian.com/books/2019/oct/14/grand-union-zadie-smith-review-short-stories. Accessed Aug 12, 2021.

Walton, James. “A New Satisfying Maturity at the Expense of Comic Zest.” *Independent.ie*. Nov 27, 2016. https://www.independent.ie/entertainment/books/book-reviews/a-new-satisfying-maturity-at-the-expense-of-comic-zest-35243102.html. Accessed August 09, 2021.

1. *Modelling Citizens: From a Digital to a Literary Public Sphere in* NW *and* Swing Time

Daniel South

Public Inquiry

Late in Zadie Smith's *Swing Time* (2016), the novel's unnamed narrator describes the entrance of digital communication into her life:

> The first email I received came from my mother. She sent it from a computer lab in the basement of University College London, where she had just taken part in a public debate, and I received it on a computer in my own college library. The content was a single Langston Hughes poem: she made me recite it in full when I called her later that evening, to prove it had arrived. (306)

In this short passage, Smith tellingly connects a number of issues. The internet is foregrounded as a tool for communication, access to which is here linked to educational institutions. By mentioning a public debate, Smith draws attention to different discursive spaces, and puts readers in mind of how the online world relates to the boundaries of public and private. The content of the email raises the question of where literature sits within this nascent digital world, and Smith's mention of Langston Hughes's poem (soon revealed to be "Dream Variations") clearly chimes with *Swing Time*'s exploration of race and cultural history. The idea that technology might not be totally trustworthy (as opposed to human memory) is also alluded to, as is the attendant fear that particular messages, ideas, and voices might be lost or forgotten in an era of digital transmission.

The complex of interconnected subjects highlighted by this passage (communication, education, technology, and identity) are among Smith's central thematic concerns, which she repeatedly revisits across her career. But excepting the theme of identity (which has been much explored in academic literature on Smith's work), the author's treatment of these issues has not yet been given thorough consideration in academic criticism. Even less explored is how these themes are frequently used to express her broader interest in the idea of the public sphere, succinctly defined by Jürgen Habermas (1974), the critical theorist most closely associated with the concept, as "the realm of our social life in which something approaching public opinion can be formed" (Habermas 1974, 49). In this chapter, I will explicate the notion of the public sphere in relation to Smith's writing, with particular attention to her treatment of digital technologies' effects on public discourse. I will outline some of the main currents of her discussions, asking what problems she raises and what solutions she suggests, with particular reference to her 2010 essay "Generation Why?", and her novels *NW* (2012) and *Swing Time*. In conclusion, I will suggest that we find in Smith's work a literary model for interactions in the public sphere which emerges from the ability of writers to effectively portray lived experience, but which is importantly underwritten by a discursive parity between writers and their readers.

Given that the concept of the public sphere will be central to this chapter's argument, it will be worth providing a brief outline of the idea to begin. In 1962, Habermas published *The Structural Transformation of the Public Sphere*, a text which has animated a half century of debate amongst political scientists, philosophers, historians, and literary scholars. *Structural Transformation* explores the historically specific bourgeois public sphere, which Habermas argues functioned as "the sphere of private people come together as a public [. . .] to engage [public authorities] in a debate over the general rules governing relations in the basically privatized but publically relevant sphere of commodity exchange and social labor" (Habermas 1989, 27). As the critical press developed throughout the seventeenth and eighteenth centuries, Habermas argues, the proliferation of salons and coffee houses across major Western European cities provided a site for bourgeois men (and select women) to debate publicly relevant ideas and opinions expounded in print. By "functionally converting the public sphere in the world of letters," the bourgeois public sphere developed, and produced a shift from the "properly political tasks of a citizenry acting in common to the more properly civic tasks of a society engaged in critical public debate" (Habermas 1989, 51–2).

The public sphere's connections with literature are central to Habermas's account of the bourgeois public sphere. Importantly, he suggests that public debates initially found their models in both print journals and domestic discussions of literature – in other words, that reading and writing historically informed and substantiated notions of publicness. Indeed, the term 'public sphere' is not to be taken as merely denoting a set of institutions where people historically came together for public discussions; it also connotes the normative ideals and practices that comprise the very idea of publicness. Habermas identifies the definitive locus of this publicness in the exercise of reason, arguing that the bourgeois public sphere was founded on the ideal of rational-critical argument, an ideal which broadly bracketed the identities of discussants in favor of a supposed meritocracy of argumentation. Given that the bourgeois public sphere was almost entirely "composed of narrow segments of the European population, mainly educated, propertied men," however, we might be more than a little sceptical about this sphere's claims to democratic legitimacy (Calhoun 1992, 3). Many critics have responded to Habermas by calling into question the efficacy, desirability, and logic of several of the normative ideals he presents, and formalizing their own models. I have argued elsewhere that Smith is one of a number of writers who take up this task themselves by highlighting in their fiction how various norms, values, ideals, and practices associated with literature might provide alternative models for publicness (South 2019). But what makes Smith's contributions to this debate so interesting is how she situates them in the context of the internet age. Most recent critical discussions of the public sphere focus on how notions of publicness are being transformed by the priorities of the internet age (Fuchs; South 2019). Smith is tuned in to these concerns, and her work highlights them to an important end, pointing to how the political public sphere could benefit from becoming more literary than digital in character.

Reduction Costs

For Smith, the rapidity with which the internet became a general purpose technology has had an inordinate impact on how we understand its role in our daily lives. In an interview given in 2010, the author pointed out that "any other revolution that took place with so many people in so little time would have a philosophy, a period of thought, a period of discussion, an argument, but the internet revolution has happened [too quickly for that]" (Smith NYPL, 2010). Smith would have internet users carefully consider their own roles in the internet revolution, and acknowledge that "most of us have just fallen into it without serious consideration." In other words, Smith believes that the internet, despite its ubiquity, has evaded adequate consideration within the public sphere, and that this should be remedied lest the technology's more creeping and insidious effects go unnoticed. Across Smith's work, she returns to one particular effect of the internet's development that can help to explain her concern further – if the internet has not been considered adequately within the public sphere, this might be because the technology has itself adversely *affected* the public sphere.

Smith's most direct exploration of this argument comes in her 2010 essay "Generation Why?," which focuses her digital skepticism on Facebook, and stages a debate that scholars of the public sphere have been having for some time, asking to what extent social media actualizes long-held aspirations for a web-based public sphere. In her essay, Smith identifies Facebook founder Mark Zuckerberg as a particular brand of cyberutopian *par excellence*, one whose obsession with 'connection' ("he uses the word 'connect' as believers use the word 'Jesus,' as if it were sacred in and of itself") establishes him as a champion of an online public sphere (Smith 2018c, 52). Yet even if Facebook's spread has undoubtedly enhanced participation in an online public sphere, Smith is concerned about its effects on the quality of discourse therein. For Zuckerberg, Smith claims, this concern is beside the point: "Connection is the goal. The quality of that connection, the quality of the information that passes through it, the quality of the relationship that connection permits – none of this is important" (52). Platforms like Facebook may look like discursive spaces, even Habermasian ones ("a uniform environment in which it genuinely doesn't matter who you are, as long as you make 'choices' "), but on such platforms these choices always mean, "finally, purchases" (59) Debate in Facebook's public sphere is something which is to be chiefly expressed through the market, whatever Zuckerberg's protestations.

Discussing the publication of "Generation Why?" during an interview, Smith outlined her interest in how social media platforms discourage discourse by robbing users of their ability to be "relational rather than performative," and fostering "an idea of being human which is one way," neglecting the fact that "real life is relational" (Smith 2010). Such a dichotomy is characteristic of Smith's writing – as she has noted herself, one of the recurrent "deep structures" of her work is that she is "always thinking about opposites" (Smith *Interview*, 2017a). Her interventions into debates about the internet's effects on public discourse are no exception: they are structured around a series of oppositions between the performative and the relational, the digital and the literary, and information and experience. From Archie's ruminations on the overwhelming nature of a data-driven society in *White Teeth* (2000, 510), to the allegorized critique of online discourse in her short story "Now More Than Ever" (2019), Smith's writing has time and again used these oppositions to question the possibility of fostering public spheres online.

It is in Smith's second novel *The Autograph Man* (2002) that we find her first sustained reference to the internet, and her first use of 'opposites' in relation to it. Smith uses the technology as a detail of protagonist Alex-Li's everyday life to comic effect:

> One day he will take advantage of this incredible resource. He will find out about ancient Babylonia and gain a working knowledge of Estonian. He will learn how to make a bomb. One day. For now, he means to head straight for his corner of the world, an imaginary auction room [...] And he will in *no way* be tempted by that friendly, clumsy woman, falling in and out of her bikini, beckoning to him from the corner of the screen... *Look, five minutes only.* (Smith 2002, 153)

Alex-Li knows that the internet could give him access to a world of knowledge (both benign and dangerous), but he defers this kind of engagement to an uncertain future, prioritizing economic profit and individual satisfaction over global and historical connection. When Alex-Li watches the pornographic pop-up, Smith includes a knowing reference that highlights a key tenet of her engagement with the internet as a topic: "Wallala leialala, cried the woman" (Smith 2002, 154). This cry is a quotation from Wagner's *Götterdämmerung*, by way of the third section of T. S. Eliot's *The Waste Land*. By incorporating this reference, Smith gestures to the network of literary influence and allusion that much of the rest of *The Autograph Man* is interested in exploring. Literature has a memory, she seems to suggest; in contrast, when Alex-Li closes his web browser, "it was gone, as if it had never been" (Smith 2002, 154). In this brief scene, Smith subtly creates one level of tension between the values associated with the digital and the literary, aligning the former with individual satisfaction and the present moment, and the latter with connection and history.

Smith builds on this alignment in her following novel, *On Beauty* (2005), a contemporary re-telling of *Howard's End* "inspired by a love of E. M. Forster" (Smith 2006, xi). Instead of beginning with Helen's letters to her sister, however, Smith brings Forster forward into the twenty-first century, and opens her novel with "Jerome's e-mails to his father" (3). *On Beauty*'s reference draws attention to the differences between communicative forms, and in a slightly later allusion to Forster's novel, Smith capitalizes on these differences to once again create a tension between the digital and the literary. Towards the end of the novel's first chapter, *On Beauty*'s Howard Belsey makes the same mistake as Mrs. Munt does in *Howard's End*, traveling to advise his son against a marriage that has already been called off. The fact that this happens despite the technological advances that could have forewarned him shows a reluctance to embrace the increasing ubiquity of digital devices not just on the character's part but on Smith's too – a feature endemic to what Toby Litt (2012) has called the "pseudo-contemporary novel." For Litt, this type of novel, "in which characters are, for some reason [...] technologically cut off," is a way for novelists to "avoid the truly contemporary (which is hyperconnectivity)." *On Beauty*'s transposition of Forster's plot, however, does not signify a *lack* of engagement with the contemporary world. Rather, it can be read as an active opposition to technology's obstinate inexorability, and another reminder of the novel form's retention of a useful sense of history. Smith knows that her world is no longer that of Forster's fiction – computers and mobile phones do appear later in *On Beauty*, assimilated into the everyday without much apparent consideration (from characters and author alike) – but her refusal to allow these devices to get in the way of her *hommage* betrays a discomfort with allowing the affordances of technology to structure her characters' encounters with the world.

In "Generation Why?," Smith articulates this discomfort more precisely, unpacking the broader ramifications of allowing digital technologies (and their attendant performativity) to set representative priorities:

> When a human being becomes a set of data on a website like Facebook, he or she is reduced. Everything shrinks. Individual character. Friendships. Language. Sensibility. [...] Software may reduce humans, but there are degrees. Fiction reduces humans, too, but bad fiction does it more than good fiction, and we have the option to read good fiction. (2018c, 58–60)

Smith here identifies reduction as an inevitability, a fundamental problem of any kind of representation. Yet if her conclusion is clear enough (good fiction does a better job of representing human beings than social media platforms like Facebook do), a question hangs over it: what constitutes the better reduction of good fiction? One answer to this question may lie in how Smith characterizes Facebook's *worse* reduction, which she suggests happens "when a human being becomes a set of data" (2018c 58). If the internet can be thought of as trying to reduce humans to a certain kind of information, perhaps literature can be thought of as trying to reduce them to another kind. If this is the case, Smith goes on to suggest in *NW* that it might be information related to *experience*.

NW wears its anxieties about representation on its sleeve. Early in the novel, one character, Leah, ruminates on narrative's relation to reduction after a charged encounter with a neighbor: "But already the grandeur of experience threatens to flatten into the conventional, into anecdote [...] Nothing survives its telling" (Smith 2012, 14). An echo of Smith's argument in "Generation Why?" can be identified here: Facebook takes representation's inherent threat to flatten experience into anecdote and makes it a certainty, denying any real chance to portray individual difference, or unsanctioned forms of community. In other words, its form is too rigid. The novel, however, is a broad church – as Smith (2011) points out in an essay on George

Eliot, "what is not universal or timeless [...] is form. Forms, styles, structures – whatever word you prefer – should change like skirt lengths" (39–40). What, then, does *NW*'s form tell us about the reality that Smith wishes to portray? The novel's shifting perspectives, multiple voices, and fluid structures might seem to represent a fractured and uncertain world. But as Joanna Biggs (2016) notes, "the prose shards of *NW* manage to tell us something about the way we tidy our lives into stories" – and, I would suggest, by attending to the internet's capacities for representation while doing so, the novel compares the kinds of stories that different technologies allow us to tell.

David James (2013) identifies the "note of artistic resignation or concession" in Leah's suggestion that nothing survives its telling, but insists that it does not mean that "Smith has given up on what the novel as a form can capture and convey with its powers of 'telling'" (James 2013, 208–9). Chapters nine and ten of *NW*'s first section provide the most overt examples of this, as Smith directly contrasts the internet and the novel form's abilities to represent characters' experiences of London. Chapter nine consists of a list of "suggested routes" and directions to take Leah "From A to B," laid out as one would be given them by an online routefinder such as Google Maps:

A5	47 mins
2.4 miles	
A5 and Salusbury Rd	50 mins
2.5 miles	
A404/Harrow Rd	58 mins
2.8 miles.	(2012, 38)

At the bottom of the route plan, readers are told that they "may find that construction projects, traffic, weather, or other events may cause conditions to differ from the map results" (Smith 2012, 38). This is a reminder of the breach between representation and the physical world that gestures towards what chapter ten immediately goes on to demonstrate further – the novel form is interested more in experience than information, and, by extension, does a better job of representing a human life.

Chapter ten, introduced as "From A to B redux", outlines the experience of Leah's journey by emphasizing sensory details, from the olfactory ("sweet stink of the hookah, couscous, kebab, exhaust fumes") to the auditory ("I give you good price, good price [...] Boomboxes just because [...] Birdsong!"). Stories emerge from the smallest details of what Leah sees ("Lone Italian, loafers, lost, looking for Mayfair"), and she is connected to memory by visual experience ("Here is the school where they stabbed the headmaster"). She is surrounded by examples of London's rich and varied cultural past in the buildings she passes ("Tudor, Modernist, post-war, pre-war, stone pineapples, stone lions, stone eagles"), and this accentuates the pluralistic make-up of contemporary London too ("Polish paper, Turkish paper, Arabic, Irish, French, Russian, Spanish, News of the World") (Smith 2012, 39–40). These two sections may seem to propose an unfair comparison – a novel is not, after all, the same thing as a map, nor would we expect (or desire) a route finder to include irrelevant information about affects in its results. Yet Smith's comparison aims to highlight the broader ramifications of privileging a data-driven and digital way of 'telling' over a literary one. Indeed, the acknowledgments in her following novel *Swing Time* can be helpful in clarifying this, as they contain "a note on geography: North London, in these pages, is a state of mind. Some streets may not appear as they do in Google Maps" (Smith 2016a, 455). Given that all of Smith's novels are set, at least in part, in North London, this note could be taken as a retrospective comment on geography applicable to each of her books, and the reference to Google Maps points to a particular idea. Smith does not concede that the streets of North London may not appear as they do *in the world*, instead framing her descriptions only in opposition to Google Maps, as for her the experiential texture of her novels provides a less reductive representation than the more utilitarian mode of information privileged online. In *Swing Time*, Smith capitalizes on the tension between digital and literary ways of telling that she has established in *NW* to point out how literature's interest in experience, and the process of reading involved in our encounters with it, can be abstracted to provide a model for a public sphere more suited than the internet is to encouraging encounters with different points of view.

Constructionist Sites

By emphasizing literature's formal ability to effectively portray individual experience, Smith also draws attention to her interest in how and why our experiences of the world differ. This interest aligns with her treatment of the public sphere in a foundational question that her work often poses: what does *difference* mean for the public sphere? In a Habermasian context, difference is irrelevant to the public sphere – it is something to be bracketed during discussion, and moved away from in the search for consensus. Yet Smith has no interest in such an approach. As she put it in a recent interview,

> it's correct to say that people's experiences absolutely matter and that they are completely various. [...] Our experiences are entirely different, and that is a revelation more important than [the idea] that we are all the same on the inside.

> [. . .] That's not true at all. In a million ways we're all incredibly different on the inside. (Smith *Document*, 2018e)

Smith recognizes that this difference extends further than our opinions – it might also have an impact on how those opinions are formed and expressed. This issue is foregrounded in *Swing Time*, where the divergent educations and experiences of the narrator and her childhood friend Tracey lead to a series of seemingly impassable misunderstandings. Smith (2013) is keen to foreground in the novel (as she did in *NW*) how "class [. . .] shapes your reality," and how education is a primary site of this difference. Implicit within the divergent lives of Tracey and *Swing Time*'s narrator is the recognition that rational-critical formulations of the public sphere can privilege certain kinds of education. "The issue here is not the inability of some groups to provide rational arguments for their beliefs," as Ferree et al. clarify, "but that narrative and other preferred modes may be unfairly devalued" (Ferree et al., 2002, 311). In *Swing Time*, Smith creates a narrator who refuses to assent to a gold standard of participation in public life, and who appears sympathetic to a constructionist approach to interaction in the public sphere, one which evinces "a strong norm of popular inclusion, which in turn serves the goals of empowerment of the marginalized and recognition of differences" (Ferree et al., 2002, 315).

Smith provides a model for such recognition in the later interactions between Tracey and *Swing Time*'s narrator. Tracey often posts messages in the kind of online chat rooms that had once been a source of hope for those tracking the emergence of a digital public sphere, but her tendency to "abus[e] anyone who did not agree with her arguments" (Smith 2016a, 440) can be read as an indictment of the state of online debate. Constructionists "do not devalue deliberation and formal argument in discourse," (Ferree et al., 311) and as such Tracey's anger and abusive tones are, quite rightly, not taken lightly by *Swing Time*'s narrator – she is "stunned by the rage" (398). When the narrator goes to confront Tracey about her abusive emails and online posts, she cannot ignore their shared personal history and divergent present circumstances, and finds it difficult to disagree with Tracey's claim that "there can't be no understanding between you and me any more! You're part of a different system now" (Smith 2016a, 405–6). But Smith's faith in the ideal of the public sphere is such that she seems unable to fully endorse Tracey's pronouncement about a lack of understanding being inevitable. Smith does not let Tracey's anger supersede the rest of her story, which comprises "a surreal mix of personal vendetta, painful memory, astute political protest and a local resident's complaints" (Smith 2016a, 399), and understandably employs an affective register to outline a "catalogue of pain: child-support woes, rent arrears, skirmishes with social workers" (446). For Smith, like most constructionists, narrative "reveals experiences based on social locations that cannot be shared fully by those who are differently situated" (Ferree et al., 313), but Smith cannot agree that this always leads *de facto* to misunderstanding. Rather, *Swing Time* gestures to the idea that the existence of 'different systems' means that the public sphere must make room for different systems of expression. The most central means of expression to a constructionist view, as mentioned above, is narrative. But Smith knows that for narrative to play a key role in the public sphere, it must be balanced by a willingness, and an ability, to *interpret* it.

Speaking in an interview about the current fractiousness of American political discourse, Smith (2018g) admits to reading "crazy, right-wing websites" in an attempt to understand the grievances of those she disagrees with. "You have to try and conceive of it," she claims – "I think you have to think of emotions as real even when they're extremely alien to you. I think that's the first step in having some form of communication." Asked if she aligns this conception specifically with writing, Smith says that "it's partly that," but reaffirms that such attempts cannot begin and end on the page, and must also be taken into everyday life as an attitude towards dialogue: "it is possible to talk to people, but you need to talk to them and you need to listen to them as well." One of the most interesting manifestations of these ideas in Smith's fiction is her recurring interest in conspiracy theories, first mooted in *NW* (164–5), but most thoroughly discussed in *Swing Time.* At one point, while *Swing Time*'s narrator is living in The Gambia to oversee the development of a school that her popstar boss, Aimee, is trying to set up, she meets "a lively young woman called Esther" (Smith 2016a, 274). Esther is amazed that Aimee "knows Jay-Z, she knows Rihanna and Beyoncé," and at one point asks, "Do you think she is Illuminati, too? Or she just is acquaintances with Illuminati?" Challenged on the veracity of claims she has read online about the Illuminati, Esther declares that "here for us it is real, because there is a lot of power there for sure" (Smith 2016a, 274).

Smith points to the value of interpreting such seemingly irrational perspectives when she links Esther's conspiracy theory to others in the novel. Tracey looks to the internet to find "truth," posting in a chat room "under the alias Truthteller_Legon" (92), first about grand conspiracies that Smith models on David Icke's 'reptoid hypothesis,' and later about "a secret eighteenth-century Bavarian sect [...] at work in the world today" (Smith 2016a, 399). Tracey's chat room contributions are clearly not deliberative, but the novel's narrator suggests that they should not be immediately dismissed within the context of the public sphere. Indeed,

> if you could put aside their insane first premise, [Tracey's posts were] striking in their detail and perverse erudition, linking many diverse historical periods and political ideas and facts [. . .] which, even in its comic wrongness, required a certain depth of study and persistent attention. (Smith 2016a, 94)

The narrator is able to "read between the lines" to find the valid message at the heart of a ridiculous story – one that she also links back to Esther's belief in the existence of the Illuminati: "Wasn't it all a way of explaining power, in the end? The power that certainly exists in the world? Which few hold and most never get near? A power my old friend must have felt, at that point in her life, she utterly lacked?" (Smith 2016a, 94). Even though conspiracy theories are not accounts of personal experience in the way that constructionist theories might expect contributions to the public sphere to be, the fact that Smith frames these stories as valid attempts to articulate both personal struggles and structural political problems, and that she suggests *reading* as the process in which this validity can be unpacked, proposes narrative as a central tenet of the contemporary public sphere.

But it is just as important that Smith has her narrator *unpack* these perspectives – if she is to some extent suggesting that the public sphere might benefit from being more literary in character, this is not just because she believes that any narrative should be taken as a permissible and helpful contribution to debate. In one interview, Smith (2017b) claims that

> we're living in an age where people feel that pathos is all you need when you make an argument – as in, 'I feel it, and so it is true.' However, an argument is not just emotion. You can feel something with incredible strength, but that's not enough. It's not true just because I feel it to be true. That world is chaos in my opinion.

In the face of this chaos, Smith (2017b) looks back to her own education for an alternative: "I was educated in things like Aristotle's idea of rhetoric [. . .] When you make an argument, you make it through Ethos, Pathos and Logos – Ethos appeals to ethics, Pathos appeals to emotion and Logos appeals to logic." Her comment suggests a more accurate way of describing the vision of the public sphere that emerges in *Swing Time*: an Aristotelian constructionism, a form of public discourse that makes room for narrative, ethical and emotional appeals, but also maintains the logical elements of a rational-critical public sphere. As Triadafilos Triadafilopoulos has claimed, "Aristotle's fusion of reason, emotion, and performance also provides us with a unique alternative to both agonistic and rational/deliberative conceptions of the public sphere" (Triadafilopoulos 1999, 774); we can identify this alternative in the forms of the public sphere that Smith portrays and alludes to.

I do not use Smith's explications of her own work here simply to bow to authorial interpretation – rather, I do so because they also represent a key part of her literary model of publicness. Smith's consideration (and reconsideration) of her ideas in public contexts represents one way in which she models this publicness, which promotes parity between the processes of writing and reading. The ways in which she discusses her own work (in essays or interviews) are key to understanding how she models certain ways of thinking critically. In this way, for Smith, literature's value to the public sphere lies as much in how it constitutes a model for interactions as in the contributions it can make to debates. Indeed, she admits that she is "less interested in convincing people of an argument than in modelling a style of thinking" (Smith *The Guardian*, 2018f). Her literary model of publicness is founded on the notion of parity between the processes of writing and reading, but to achieve this equality both writer and reader must recognize their own perspectives as contingent. For Smith, this recognition of difference can embed relationality into the public sphere: the "extension away from yourself, into other people," she suggests, "is maybe what fiction could model as a kind of citizenship behaviour," in an attempt to build a "coalition across difference" (Smith *YouTube*, 2018a). By asking what difference means for the public sphere, then, Smith also implicitly asks how the public sphere might enable us to navigate, and indeed to embrace, such difference in public life.

Feel Free to Change Your Mind

In the foreword to her second essay collection, *Feel Free*, Smith suggests that

> essays about one person's affective experience have, by their very nature, not a leg to stand on. All they have is their freedom. And the reader is likewise unusually free, because I have absolutely nothing over her, no authority. She can reject my feelings at every point, she can say: 'No, I have never felt that' or 'Dear Lord, the thought never crossed my mind!' (2018b, xi)

The imperative title of Smith's collection is revealed here as a directive for both herself and her readers, a description of the free interpretation enacted at both ends of her creative process. For Smith, it is of the utmost importance that we recognize "that reading involves all the same liberties and exigencies as writing" – we can in fact understand this balance as the basis of her literary model of publicness (2018b xii). Her 2017 essay "Getting In and Out," provides an apposite statement of this model. Writing in opposition to a public call to have a painting of Emmet Till by a white artist, Dana Schutz, destroyed, Smith suggests that

> art is a traffic in symbols and images, it has never been politically or historically neutral [...]. Each individual example has to be *thought through*, and we have every right to include such considerations in our evaluations of art [...]. The solution remains as it has always been. Get out (of the gallery) or deeper in (to the argument). Write a screed against it. Critique the hell out of it. Tear it to shreds in your review or paint another painting in response. (2018d, 220–222)

Smith asserts her faith in the power of the public sphere in relation to art here, and in doing so combines her insistence upon individual perspective with a recognition of the importance of collaborative reflection and debate. Indeed, Smith presents the affordance to readers or spectators of the same rights as artists as the very thing which underwrites any important issue's consideration in a piece of art.

Smith's approach, of course, isn't without its detractors – and, characteristically for an author open to changing her mind, Smith herself is one of them. In "Getting In and Out," Smith points out that when artworks like Schutz's are "facilely celebrated as proof of the autonomy of art," this is "more often than not hoary old white privilege dressed up as aesthetic theory" (Smith 2018d, 220). When asked about the impulse to restrict the treatment of certain subjects to those with direct experience of them, however, Smith's ambivalence is clear: "I don't think it's the worst crime [...] but I don't think it's ideal" (2018e). Smith's ambivalence about what she calls "an artist's right to a particular subject" actually structures "Getting In and Out," manifesting in the fact that much of the essay's treatment of the issue comprises questions rather than positions (Smith 2018d, 218). Her questions are mainly phrased as responses to a letter sent to the curators of the Whitney Biennial by artist Hannah Black, who called for the destruction of Schutz's painting. Smith focuses in particular on one part of the letter, Black's argument that "the subject matter is not Schutz's; white free speech and white creative freedom have been founded on the constraint of others, and are not natural rights" (Black, qtd. in Smith 2018d, 218). In the interview I cited earlier, Smith suggests that thinking of the issue of an artist's right to a particular subject in terms of *individual* rights misses the point: "the question of duties is more important than the question of individual rights because individual rights echo a kind of capitalist dogma [...]: What's accrued to me? What can I get? What am I owed? That, I find, is a depressing political place" (Smith *Document*, 2018e). Rather, if Smith wants all subjects to be available to all minds, it is because there exist "collective duties" in need of renewal, and "structural inequalities" that require collective attention (2108e). An etic perspective (that from outside a particular social group) should never override an emic one (from within that group) outright, but Smith believes that the former should not be dismissed out of hand, either – rather, "each individual example has to be *thought through*" (2018d, 220).

Throughout her career, Smith has herself claimed the right to explore any number of subjects and subjectivities, thinking of herself "explicitly as a voyeur, somebody who wants to be inside other people's lives" (Smith *New Statesman*, 2016b). Despite this, her work has been frequently considered by many critics biographically, through the lens of her celebrity. Given that her high-profile career has been conducted in the public eye even since before the publication of *White Teeth*, this is perhaps unsurprising. Since that time, when she was heralded as "the first publishing sensation of the millennium," public discourse about Smith has often centered as much on the author as on her work (Merritt 2000). As Philip Tew points out, the author's celebrity status influenced "the ideological assumptions and presumptions of many academic critics" writing about *White Teeth* in particular, who often adopted "the parameters underpinning the 'public,' initially commercially driven discourse which memorialized the meaning of both the first novel and its author in culturally symbolic terms" (Tew 118). Tew here usefully highlights how Smith's reception can tell us something about the links between authorship, publicness, and celebrity, and reminds us that the market often holds great sway over public discussions of literature.

We can in fact return to Facebook for a neat example of Smith's place within the public sphere. Smith's American publisher, Penguin Press, runs a Facebook page on the author's behalf, dedicated to marketing her work. One post on the individualized page advertises her second essay collection, *Feel Free*, with a quotation from Smith's essay "The I Who Is Not Me": "For me fiction is a way of asking: what if things were other than they are? And a central component of that is to ask: what if I was different than I am? I have always found the practice of writing fiction far more an escape from self than an exploration of it" (Penguin Press 2017). To the left of the quotation is a picture of the book's cover, emblazoned with her name; on the right, Facebook's commenting interface, a picture of Smith, and a reminder that the new collection is forthcoming. This image sums up how Smith's writing is often caught between the concerns of the market and the perceptions of the public, and serves as a prompt for us to pay more attention to where the ideas that she explores sit in this relationship. Her writing situates her as central to contemporary fiction's exploration of the public sphere, and instantiates a model of literary publicness where authority emerges not solely from the author figure, but from the exchange of ideas between writers and readers. The result of this work, Smith hopes, is that we will all feel free to change our minds whenever we need to.

Works Cited

Biggs, J. (2016). "Whomph!" *London Review of Books*, 1 December, 2016. http://www.lrb.co.uk/v38/n23/joanna-biggs/whomph

Calhoun, C. (1992). "Introduction: Habermas and the Public Sphere." In *Habermas and the Public Sphere*, edited by Craig Calhoun, 1–48. Cambridge: The MIT Press.

Ferree, M. M., Gamson, W. A., Gerhards J., & Rucht, D. (2002). "Four Models of the Public Sphere in Modern Democracies." *Theory and Society*, 31(3), 289–324. doi: https://doi.org/10.1023/A:1016284431021

Fuchs, C. (2014). *Social Media: A Critical Introduction*. London: Sage Publications.

Habermas, J. (1974). "The Public Sphere: An Encyclopedia Article (1964)." Translated by Sara Lennox and Frank Lennox. *New German Critique* 3, 49–55. DOI: https://doi.org/10.2307/487737

———. (1989). *The Structural Transformation of the Public Sphere: An Inquiry into a Category of Bourgeois Society*. Translated by Thomas Burger with Frederick Lawrence. Cambridge: Polity. First published 1962.

James, David. (2013). "Wounded Realism." *Contemporary Literature*, 54(1), 204–214. doi: https://doi.org/10.1353/cli.2013.0000

Litt, T. (2012). "The Reader and Technology." *Granta*, April 10, 2012. http://www.granta.com/The-Reader-and-Technology

Merritt, S. (2000). "She's young, black, British – and the first publishing sensation of the Millennium." *The Guardian*, January 16, 2000. https://www.theguardian.com/books/2000/jan/16/fiction.zadiesmith

Penguin Press. (2017). "Feel Free, Zadie's new collection of essays, is coming 2/6." *Facebook*, December 28, 2017. https://goo.gl/9nh7q3

Smith, Z. (2000). *White Teeth*. London: Hamish Hamilton.

———. (2002). *The Autograph Man*. London: Penguin.

———. (2006). *On Beauty*. London: Penguin. First published 2005.

———. (2010). "Live from the NYPL: Zadie Smith." Interview by P. Holdengräber. *New York Public Library*, November 22, 2010. Audio, 1:35:00. http://www.nypl.org/audiovideo/zadie-smith?nref=90281

———. (2011). "Middlemarch and Everybody." In *Changing My Mind: Occasional Essays*, 28–40. London: Penguin.

———. (2012). *NW*. London: Penguin.

———. (2013). "Guardian Books podcast: Zadie Smith on NW." Interview by John Mullan. *The Guardian Books Podcast*, July 26, 2013. Audio, 34:00. http://www.theguardian.com/books/audio/2013/jul/26/zadie-smith-nw-london-podcast

———. (2016a). *Swing Time*. London: Hamish Hamilton.

———. (2016b). "'Trump is a Great Opportunity For Us Writers': Zadie Smith On Fighting Back." Interview by Tom Gatti. *New Statesman*, December 2, 2016, https://www.newstatesman.com/culture/books/2016/12/trump-great-opportunity-us-writers-zadie-smith-fighting-back

———. (2017a). "George Saunders." *Interview*, February 15, 2017, https://www.interviewmagazine.com/culture/george-saunders

———. (2017b). "An Interview With Zadie Smith." Interview by Lisa Sproull. *Cult MTL*, October 26, 2017. http://www.cultmontreal.com/2017/10/zadie-smith-interview/

———. (2018a) "A Conversation between Authors Zadie Smith, Yaa Gyasi, and Courtney Martin." Interview by Courtney Martin. *YouTube*, November 19, 2018. Video, 22:54. https://www.youtube.com/watch?v=S4g-_hir2AE

———. (2018b). "Foreword." In *Feel Free: Essays*, xi–xii. London: Hamish Hamilton.

———. (2018c). "Generation Why?" In *Feel Free: Essays*, 45–63. London: Hamish Hamilton. First published 2010.

———. (2018d). "Getting In and Out." In *Feel Free: Essays*, 212–224. London: Hamish Hamilton. First published 2017.

———. (2018e). "Novelists Édouard Louis and Zadie Smith on writing in a distracting political present." Interview by N. T. Pemberton. *Document*, April 12, 2018, http://www.documentjournal.com/2018/04/novelists-edouard-louis-and-zadie-smith-on-writing-in-a-distracting-political-present

———. (2018f). "Zadie Smith: 'I have a very messy and chaotic mind'." *The Guardian*, January 21, 2018. http://www.theguardian.com/books/2018/jan/21/zadie-smith-you-ask-the-questions-self-doubt

———. (2019). "Now More Than Ever." In *Grand Union: Stories*, 225–238. London: Hamish Hamilton.

South, D. (2019). *Literature and the Public Sphere in the Internet Age*. Unpublished PhD Eng. thesis. University of York, UK. Retrieved from White Rose eTheses Online: http://etheses.whiterose.ac.uk/24438/

Tew, P. (2009). *Zadie Smith (New British Fiction)*. Basingstoke: Palgrave Macmillan.

Triadafilopoulos, T. (1999). "Politics, Speech, and the Art of Persuasion: Toward an Aristotelian Conception of the Public Sphere." *The Journal of Politics* 61(3), 741–757. doi: https://doi.org/10.2307/2647826

2. *Zadie Smith's George Eliot's Spinoza: The Ethics of Austere Realism*

James Arnett

In the Foreword to *Changing My Mind*, Zadie Smith writes, "When you are first published at a young age, your writing grows with you – and in public," as a way to describe how her style grew out of and away from the early success of her polyvocal, carnivalesque, Dickensian maximalism of *White Teeth* (*Changing* 2009, xiii). In these critical and self-reflective essays, Smith begins to articulate a more evolved theory of the purpose and value of fiction, and a central essay in the collection, "*Middlemarch* and Everybody," outlines what she sees is the genealogy for her new mode. She remarks George Eliot's growth and identifies with her growth from young adulthood into maturity, with its attendant shedding of absolutes; "the young Eliot could only exult in the perfect truths we glean from certain books in our libraries; the mature Eliot has learned to have sympathy for the stumbling errors of human beings" (*Changing* 2009, 32). If readers, Smith gleans from Eliot, could but spend their time tarrying with the errors of our acquaintances and fellows, we might come to a more patient understanding of man's desire to do and be good, even when he might fall short. This tenderness for human error inflects Smith's writing more and more through the twenty-first century.

Smith's writing takes on a real sympathy for both the tragic and the comic in our stumbling human behavior, culminating in her short essay collection, *Intimations* (2020), on the [as of press, still ongoing] Covid-19 pandemic. In *NW*, Nathan Bogle tragically stumbles through the text, buffeted by socioeconomic and social violences, and subjected to ideologies of exclusion and impoverishment. On the other hand, more patently comic characters like Andrew in "The Embassy of Cambodia" – full of bluster, malapropism, and flawed patriarchal reasoning – are deemed no less worthy of our bemused respect. "Experience, for Eliot, was a powerful way of knowing,"

Smith limns, because "experience transforms perspective, and transformations in perspective, to Eliot, constitute real changes in the world" (*Changing* 2009, 32). Literature is key to this shift in orientation and affect that can lead to transformation in material circumstances precisely because it doles out its lessons in sympathy, and because its embrace of the ambivalence of human character replaces morality with ethics.

Before George Eliot (became George Eliot and) came to writing fiction, Marian Evans came to philosophy from philology, having taught herself the classical and modern European languages, including Hebrew. Evans was a voracious intellectual who grew out and away from her Evangelical religious education and background with the help of lifelong friends Charles and Cara Bray, who introduced her to the work of Feuerbach and David Friedrich Strauss (which Evans translated from the German and published under her name) and, ultimately, to Spinoza. Eliot was drawn to the pragmatic geometries and rationalities of Spinoza's proven method, and her translation of Strauss, Feuerbach, and Spinoza added greatly to the growing body of materialist and ersatz-atheist philosophies of the nineteenth century.

Evans's translation of Spinoza, however, never saw the light of day, in spite of her privately signaled agreement with its content.[1] Evans's translation was galvanized by her partner George Henry Lewes's work in the area of natural philosophy, which had already brought him to Spinoza. Lewes's iconoclastic genealogy of philosophy attempted to recuperate Spinoza from the margins to which he had been long consigned by previous readers and scholars, for the sins of presumptive heresy, atheism, and/or pantheism.[2] Spinoza had been, before and after Evans picked him up, a dangerous thinker; and Evans's close reading of his philosophy – in Latin, Greek, and Hebrew, no less – helped to facilitate Marian Evans's evolution from a trust in Christlike kindness and morality to a faith in (secular) ethical fellow-feeling.

Eliot's daring life, and relationship with Lewes, compels Zadie Smith to marvel in her essay, "*Middlemarch* and Everybody," her relationship with Lewes was "exactly the right kind of *conatus*: a power-strengthening union characterized by joy" (*Changing* 2009, 36). It was a corollary benefit that the materialist philosophical translations of Evans were also not directly linked to her fictional output – for Spinoza has never sat easily with the religious, with scholars of philosophy, with philosophers themselves. Indeed, Smith acutely notes that Spinoza served as a "riposte…to the arid rigors of her family's Methodism," and that Eliot's "rejection of the organized church, so horrifying to her family, was really a turning away from false, abstract moral values" (*Changing* 2009, 36). In a collection of essays entitled *Changing My Mind*, we can read here, too, Smith's anxiety to demonstrate that not only she, but her writing, has grown.

For reasons that still make dogmatic religious readers uncomfortable with Spinoza, the immanently material(ist) god-world that Spinoza describes encompasses the impingement and co-composition of all things, and thus in many ways obviates the anthropomorphic ideal of God proffered in most religions at the time. Spinoza describes a world composed of substance, each of which is "necessarily infinite" (Spinoza 1994, I.P8), that "God, *or* a substance consisting of infinite attributes, each of which expresses eternal and infinite essence, necessarily exists" (Spinoza 1994, I.P11), and cutting to the chase, thereby demonstrates that "Whatever is, is in God, and nothing can be or be conceived without God" (Spinoza 1994, I.P15). This immanence engenders a complex affective ethics requiring us to improve our knowledge of the world (as it is) in order to understand better, and thus more ethically, our responsibility to ourselves and any other, given our composition of God in/as substance. Moreover, and accordingly, all living things possess a *conatus* – a drive to persist in the world. We thereby innately share a common and concomitant liveness and must thereby understand that each subject seeks its own furtherance. Inasmuch as we can recognize our own *conatus* and desire, we must respect (the existence of) others('), leading contemporary thinkers like Hardt and Negri, Balibar, and others, to remark that Spinoza's ethics is conducive to the commons, and communism (in political forms). As Spinoza reflects in Section IV of the *Ethics*, "Man, I say, can wish for nothing more helpful to the preservation of his being than that all should so agree in all things that the minds and bodies of all would compose, as it were, one mind and one body; that all should strive together, as far as they can, to preserve their being; and that all, together, should seek for themselves the common advantage of all" (Spinoza 1994, IV P.19).[3] In other words, knowledge, distilled from experience (of others) augments our capacity to be and share good(s).

There's no denying the genealogical connection between Spinoza's humane philosophy and Eliot's humanely rendered literary realism.[4] One of the plain appeals of Spinoza's philosophy is his generosity, the kind that echoes Eliot's pleasing observation that it is "just as well" that we walk about the world "well-wadded with stupidity." Both recognize that we humans are a funny lot, perhaps perfectible but almost never so. As Moira Gatens remarks, quoting Spinoza, he takes "'great pains not to laugh at human actions, or mourn them, or curse them, but only to understand them'," an "attention and deliberation" characterized "by the capacity to attend to, and to deliberate on, the value for a joyful life of the things and beings and contexts with which we are always, and necessarily, in relation" (Gatens 2019). In this way, Spinoza describes our obligation to our impingement on others – that we are always *in relation* to others, and accordingly, bear responsibility to them and ourselves vis-à-vis them. Anthony Uhlmann, at this intersection, argues that fiction's exemplarity can aid philosophy, leveraging projection as a mechanism for the cultivation of sympathy. As Gatens explains, "The assertion that fellow feeling is the only 'universal bond' is, for Eliot, a [fundamental] given [in Spinoza]. She had faith in that bond to found and nourish human community. The affective bonds between people depend on their ways of life, their shared histories, and their shared pleasures and pains. The imaginative and emotional lives of people are thus the basis from which fellow feelings might grow" (Gatens 2012). Thus, Eliot understands that literature has the capacity, through the work of imagination and projection, to cultivate our empathy for others and thereby increase each others' capacity and desire for good in the world.

"It's a poor look-out" after all, Adam Bede remarks, "to come into the world to make your fellow-creatures worse off instead o' better" (Eliot 2008, 182). We are all of us trying our best to do our best by, and for, ourselves – but we do not always act on the best information or understanding of our situation, and how our situation impacts or affects others. Smith's shorthand rendering of this dynamic is analogous, if limited: "From Spinoza, Eliot took the idea that the good we strive for should be nothing more than 'what we certainly know will be useful to us,' not a fixed point, no specific moral system, not, properly speaking, a morality at all. . .Instead, wise men pursue what is best in and *best for* their own natures" (*Changing* 2009, 35). In this way, we see the general applicability of the universality of Spinoza's framework – that it is tailored in formula to the particularity of the subject and their capacity for wisdom and their individuated will and inclinations.

But, we are all of us invariably erring, as Eliot reminds us over and over again, just "great beautiful dogs," really, like Fred Vincy, yearning for a caress and a kind word. In *Adam Bede,* Dinah's last-minute counsel of Hetty Poyser situates us in this fallen world: "Because, dear, trouble comes to us all in this life: we set our hearts on things which it isn't God's will for us to have, and then we go sorrowing; the people we love are taken from us, and we can joy in nothing because they are not with us; sickness comes, and we faint under the burden of our feeble bodies; we go astray and do wrong, and bring ourselves into trouble with our fellow-men. There is no man or woman born into this world to whom some of these trials do not fall" (Eliot 2008, 175). We always mean to do our best, but whether or not that best is the best for us or others is not always discernible to us. This universality of human experience dictates our experiences of success and failure, pleasure and pain, joy and sorrow.[5] We cannot know in advance what may be asked of us by others, what particular responsibility we may bear toward others; we can merely know *that* we are beholden to any/other person. Hence – "*Middlemarch* and Everybody." In a sly moment early in *NW*, Smith depicts Leah's solipsistic, doodling mantra, "I am the sole author [of my own destiny]" being interrupted by the bang on the door of a desperate neighborhood grifter (Smith 2013, 2–6). Leah's hand-wringing, should-I-or-shouldn't-I help her, elucidates the immanent Spinozist principle of charity without pity or condition.

Moreover, Smith cites Eliot's "practical morality" as easily educable and evolving, as in Adam Bede's folksy observation that "The more knowledge a man has, the better he'll do's work; and feeling's a sort o' knowledge" (Eliot 2008, 556). Adam unconsciously reproduces the thrust of Spinoza's ethics – that because we live, and are possessed of/by *conatus,* we do what we believe is best for ourselves, and our ability to effect good is contingent on the relative truth value of our knowledge of the world. Miriam Henson remarks, *a propos* of *Middlemarch,* that where Spinoza and Eliot diverge is that "Eliot chooses to encourage a compassion based on feeling, rather than that exercised by Spinoza's ideal rational man," and while this might be true of Eliot's early works – it becomes clear, as I have argued elsewhere, that by *Daniel Deronda* (at least) feeling is only the catalyst to our increased desire to augment our understanding in the service of ethical efficacy. Our inescapably first-person consciousness and conscience, our perpetual self-regard, need not be abandoned (as in models of selfless Christian martyrdom), and in fact cannot be abandoned, just understood, and trained to attend to others in addition to self. Eliot's famous image in *Middlemarch* of the polished pier-glass, scored by the maid's scrubbing, demonstrates our essential self-centeredness: even though the lines go in all directions, once illuminated by a candle, they all appear to point to the lighted center (of self and gaze) (*Middlemarch* 264). Nevertheless, we must recall that every other subject has an "equivalent centre of self," a first-personhood and subjectivity (*Middlemarch 211*). Even in Eliot's earliest fiction, her narrator urges, "surely the only true knowledge of our fellow-man is that which enables us to feel with him – which gives us a fine ear for the heart-pulses that are beating under the mere clothes of circumstance and opinion" (*Scenes* 267).

The labor of literature is to slow down the frame enough for the reader to see, and the writer to record, as many of these intersecting and impinging, contingent affects. Smith unstintingly praises Eliot, "With a scalpel Eliot dissects degrees of human velleity, finding the conscious action hidden within the impulse hidden within the desire hidden within the will tucked away deep inside the decision that we have obfuscated even from ourselves" (*Changing* 2009, 33). Eliot's excavations of human motivations prove that because we can never know all of the (self-serving) reasons we do what we do that we must also be (implicitly) as kind to others as we would want them to be to us. Eliot's steadfast depiction of 'us' humans as lovable in spite of our failures, is everywhere mimicked in Smith's later work, which is more careful in its judgments than her earlier work. There is no black or white, as Leah learns in *NW*; indeed, as she learns, the world is composed of countless microaffects, consequences, and gradations in/of knowledge that alter our place within it perpetually and imperceptibly. Eliot maintained a leveling gaze at her creations, refusing to insist on the hierarchies its own characters would, and Smith applauds the fact that "all were equal, and of equal interest, and worthy of an equal number of pages. All her people are striving toward the fullest truth, the least partial good" (*Changing* 2009, 35). Some of this is amply explained in a wistful remark Smith makes of Eliot's milieu, because "For Eliot, in 1870, people are still all that people really have," which although Smith does not contrast this to the current moment, it is clear that is no longer the case. It's this "hopeful creed" of Eliot's – that we are all each other has – "that has bonded readers to Eliot for over a century," in no small part because of the implicit nostalgia for human connection depicted therein, because "right now the news cycle is moving so fast that it feels the wheels might come off" (*Feel Free* 32). We are now globalized subjects in a capitalistically technologized world; we may have each other, but we've also welcomed new barriers to human connection under the aegis of maximal and perpetual human connection, and fetishized and weaponized self-awareness and self-care.

In a critical evaluation of Smith's *NW*, David Marcus in *Dissent* magazine praises the evolution of Smith's socioeconomic consciousness in her later work; increasingly, Smith demonstrates a closer attention to the material social and ideological forces that constrain the self-realization of her characters – working class or poor and bourgeois, citizen and immigrant alike. This is no easy task in a contemporary era characterized by its fraught interconnectedness and globalization. "For what makes life so ambiguous and morally complex today is that our very prosperity rests upon distant but not unknown inequalities and traumas happening elsewhere, to other people. The true turn toward ethics, toward our sacred human complexities, means mining not only the ways in which we feel but also exposing the stratified ways we live" (Marcus 2013). Marcus calls this "austere realism," but it is also an attempt to wrestle the ethical lineage of literary realism into alignment with contemporary conditions, as Smith herself argues in "*Middlemarch* and Everybody." According to Marcus's Marxist-inflected reading, Smith's later fictions become, in a way, "a catalogue of economic austerity: a work of socio-psychological genius that registers the psychic and material shocks of those left behind in Northwest London – those living in the type of public housing familiar on both sides of the Atlantic, where the buildings have regal names but also cracked-cement lawns and boarded-up windows" (Marcus 2013). Austere realism, with its thoroughly unromantic depiction of ideological, structural, and material forces that impinge upon, form and deform, our character(s), aligns ungauzily with Spinoza's description of human knowledges (and ignorances) and capacity to affect and be, or become, more ethical. In this manner, Smith tries to articulate a praxis of generosity and sympathy in the face of growing political polarization, the evaporation of public commons and goods, the identity and citizenship debates around Brexit, and a growing populist isolationism in world politics.

Contemporarily to Eliot, Elizabeth Gaskell advised, in her earnest Preface to *Mary Barton,* that we indulge our interest in our fellow-men, precisely the ones who "elbow [us] daily in the busy streets," and therefrom cultivate our sympathy with their suffering at the hands of the prosperous, whose ownership of capital and labor determine the poor working lives and conditions of which the common man complains (Gaskell 1996, 3). Smith adapts Gaskell's (and Eliot's) social realism to an era where such connections to the common public Other are often obscured by the spatial organization and social hierarchization of capital – man's arms'-length distance from man vis-à-vis technologies like the cellphone, or chip-and-pin card, which hold other bodies at a literal and virtual distance from the insulated self. But this austere realism is just a literary realism for a contemporary neoliberal era of financialization and globalization, and its attendant whiplashing backlash. Indeed, in "Embassy of Cambodia," Fatou, an African immigrant nanny serves the Derawal family (themselves a second generation immigrant family from the tatters of Britain's twentieth century empire) in a tiny room in their London home. The Derawal matriarch holds and hides Fatou's passport, denies her full wages (claiming that room and board dominate her earnings), and otherwise surveil and afflict Fatou. "It was not the first time that Fatou had wondered if she herself was a slave," the collective narrator observes ("Embassy" 17–19). Not much happens in the story – refreshingly so, given the plotted and plodding maximalism of her earlier works – and that is also the formal point: the novel is determined by the limitations of Fatou's agency and mobility. Fatou, throughout, walks to and from a neighborhood gym and swimming pool, past the unlikely Embassy of Cambodia, listening to the "pock" and "smash" of a shuttlecock in what feels like an unceasing game of badminton behind its walls. The novella is broken into pieces, headed by a permanently losing score, reminding us that Fatou, like the shuttlecock, is the object batted back and forth by the forces of globalized capitalism, having reduced her to the status of immigrant and human resource.[6] By framing the whole story around Fatou, the bourgeois reader's hunger for action is stymied by the "profound fatuity of twenty-first century bourgeois existence" (*Changing* 2009, 80). Moreover, the dynamics of Fatou's attunement, of her listening over the wall of the Embassy, or our/narratorial watching the street from the balcony, speaks to the tightening net of British identity and citizenship in an anti-immigrant surveillance state.

Who should we care for, or care about, Smith asks us – those that care for us? Fatou's Nigerian friend Andrew posits a theory of the limits of sympathy, giving more concrete voice to the narrator who hedges and offers that our own self-imposed limits of sympathy are self-protective – there are so many of our own "necessary tasks [and] occasional pleasures" to consider ("Embassy" 23). Andrew's theory suggests that ethnic belonging or national identity, as determined first by family belonging, inscribe the circle around our attention and sympathy: "Who cried most for Jesus? His mother. Who cries most for you? Your father. It's very logical, when you break it down. The Jews cry for the Jews. The Russians cry for the Russians. We cry for Africa, because we are Africans," but even that has limits, he rejoins, because he'd still "cheer" for Nigeria over Ivory Coast ("Embassy" 27).

Smith's more recent story "The Lazy River," in *Grand Union,* instead of foregrounding the immigrant shadow-subjects inside a globalized Britain, depicts the sunset of British mobility and extraversion under the tightening conditions begotten by Brexit. The entrapped Fatou, is replaced by the self-entrapped, self-netted Brexiteered subject. Also employing the collective first-person narrator of "Embassy," "The Lazy River" 's 'we' straddles reality and metaphoricity: she's talking to/about us! It is "us," and us, and is also "our"-selves' other. The story's collective narrator confesses that perhaps we're just insufficiently interested in others at the end of the day: "No, we have not seen the Moorish ruins. Nor will we be traveling into those bare, arid mountains. Not one soul among us had read the recent novel set right here, in Almería, nor do we have any intention of doing so," the collective narrator remarks of our Spanish vacation (*Union* 2019, 27). "We" are ultimately steadfastly uninterested, and frankly so, in anything but the passivity of vacation, of leisure, of privilege, of the refusal to recognize others and otherness, and of inertia – we are here to be served. We are meant to feel uncomfortable being spoken about, meant to feel uncomfortable at the possibility of seeing our/selves in this picture, but "We're submerged, all of us," in the 'lazy river.' "You, me, the children, our friends, their children, everybody else. Sometimes we get out. . .never for very long" (*Grand Union* 2019, 25) – we are stuck in a circle of self-regard. The lazy river itself becomes a metaphor for our attentional circle – like the circles drawn around what and whom is worthy of attention and regard in "The Embassy of Cambodia." The lazy river is also the inertia of the decision to "leave" vis-à-vis Brexit – the long afterlife of half-life in the antechamber of the break. We may pull ourselves out of the lazy river, but "never for very long, [and] then," after that, "we all climb back into the metaphor" anyway (*Grand Union* 2019, 25). "The Lazy River" is "a circle, it is wet, it has an artificial current," and this contemporary leisure-time invention is "a metaphor and at the same time a real body of artificial water" (*Grand Union* 2019, 25–26). Brexit, inasmuch as it is a political line drawn around British citizenship and British identity, is reflected in the mechanics of this upper-class frivolity: we are submerged, we are swept into and with the current; we cannot fight it, and "even if you don't move you will get somewhere and then return to wherever you started" (*Grand Union* 2019, 25) in an endlessly repeating return that performs stagnation. To be swept along its current is to be swept along the inevitable path to Britain's self-isolation and forceful renegotiation of identity, its return to loneness, isolation from the globalized world order.

"Some take this principle of universal flow to an extreme," 'we' say, these people "play[ing] dead," discovering nevertheless that "even a corpse goes round" (*Grand Union* 2019, 26). You can refuse to fight, or accede to conditions, and even so, you can't do anything to extricate yourself from the dubious circle; "A few people. . .make a point of turning the other way," but "It's a pose; it can't last long," and they, too, fail to make headway against the current we've built for, and against, ourselves (*Grand Union* 2019, 26). The current is all-encompassing, its pull too hard to break once we have decided to enter it – as is the weight of the Brexit decision to "leave" the EU as it dragged out through endless (re)negotiations in the long duration after the Brexit vote concluded.

But just outside of the literal frame of the Spanish resort and its lazy river, outside of its "polytunnels," the plexiglass containers shielding guests from the elements, "we saw the Africans who work here, alone or in pairs, riding their bicycles in the merciless sun, moving between the polytunnels" (*Grand Union* 2019, 27). The lazy river, the resort, the polytunnels describe the literal infrastructure of the world as the attentional circles we erect out of and for self-interest. The seasonal workers, liminal and limited by their immigrant status, are outside of the borders of the constructed environment of the twenty-first century. They are exposed to the heat, and to the indifferent view of those being catered to, and in the wavering heat of midday, are replaced in the narrator's field of vision by a "little punnet of baby tomatoes, wrapped in plastic," emblazoned with "PRODUCT OF SPAIN" and a barcode (*Grand Union* 2019, 27–28). In this moment, the criticality of the immigrant African laborer collapses into the contemporary agricultural commodity their labor enables; and the barcoded tomatoes replicate the surveillance state data-based tracking of barcoded and enumerated immigrants. The State is watching 'them' so 'we' don't have to.

Eliot, however, argues that we should see them, and that the work of art is not to exclude those menial architects of our social infrastructure, but to set them near the center, where they already are. Eliot articulates this powerfully and famously in Chapter 17 of *Adam Bede*. In it, she calls for writers to set aside the perfect Madonnas and exemplars of moral virtue, and instead call forth "those old women scraping carrots with their work-worn hands, those heavy clowns taking holiday in a dingy pot-house, those rounded backs and stupid weather-beaten faces that have bent over the spade and done the rough work of the world" (Eliot 2008, 196). Eliot's weather-beaten faces transmute into the melting Amy Winehouse face of the shin tattoos of pasty vacationing Britons; "and we do not judge him, not at all, how could we? We do not have so many saints of Amy's caliber left to us; we cherish her" (*Grand Union* 2019, 27). Smith, picking up the parlance of our times, likens these two gape-mouthed white British bodies (the tattoo, the tattooed) – not unlike the "gormless" old woman on the balcony in Willesden in "Embassy" – and both questions our commitments to honoring "our" "own," and in her citation of the immigrant others outside the polytunnels, challenges us to recognize an other as an "equivalent centre of self." From this vantage point, Smith wonders if it is easier to "come to the conclusion that human nature is lovable… by living a great deal among people more or less commonplace and vulgar, of whom you would perhaps hear nothing very surprising if you were to inquire about them in the neighborhoods where they dwelt" (Eliot 2008, 201). The African migrant workers transiting to and from their jobs serving vacationers are as worthy of remark as the ersatz center of our lazy attention, the British holidaymaker. What do we know about our neighbors, in whosever neighborhood we find ourselves in?

"On the way back to the hotel," "The Lazy River"'s narrator remarks after venturing just beyond one bubble (the resort) to another (the boardwalk) that exposes her to the physical world (she cringes under the "ever-warming temperature, and infinite horizons, reminders of death" [31]), "we stop by the ladies who plait hair, one from Senegal and the other from the Gambia" (*Grand Union* 2019, 33). These women – later named, Mariatou and Cynthia – are always-already exposed to the buffeting beams and waves of the elemental world, consigned to plying their trade outdoors. Moreover, they have not picked a geopolitically easy route to self-sufficiency: the coast of Spain is "even more treacherous than the one between Libya and Lampedusa, by which route they came" (*Grand Union* 2019, 33). In response to our tentative questions of them, Mariatou says, "It is hard in Spain... 'Very hard.' 'To live well?' Cynthia adds, pulling our daughters hair, making her yelp, 'is not easy.' " (*Grand Union* 2019, 33)[7] The narrator, for what it is worth, is asking these immigrant laborers to not only perform affective labor in the form of hair-braiding, but affective labor in the form of self-narration and self-explanation, revealing the double bind of immigrant subjects in a neoliberal attention economy: beholden both to working and to explaining themselves.

Lest we forget that all of our lives are propped up by the under acknowledged labor that reproduces our social and material infrastructure, Eliot's narrator in *Adam Bede* passionately intones,

> It is so needful we should remember their existence, else we may happen to leave them quite out of our religion and philosophy and frame lofty theories which only fit a world of extremes. Therefore, let Art always remind us of them; therefore let us always have men ready to give the loving pains of a life to the faithful representing of commonplace things—men who see beauty in these commonplace things, and delight in showing how kindly the light of heaven falls on them. There are few prophets in the world; few sublimely beautiful women; few heroes. I can't afford to give all my love and reverence to such rarities: I want a great deal of those feelings for my every-day fellow-men, especially for the few in the foreground of the great multitude, whose faces I know, whose hands I touch, for whom I have to make way with kindly courtesy. (Eliot 2008, 196–197)

In this manifesto for the ethics of literary realism, Eliot enjoins us to marshal our sympathy not for those whose power, privilege, or beauty compels us to attend them, but rather to the many whose faces we see in our actual lives who are not nearly as successful in compelling our sympathies. As S. Pearl Brilmyer argues, in *Middlemarch*, Eliot shows us as moral creatures to be far more plastic than we might even give ourselves credit for; her "materialist characterology implies that character traits and behaviors emerge neither through the unwilled unfolding of a preformed nature nor through the expression of the individual will, but *relationally*" (Brilmeyer, 2015 63). Moreover, "although Eliot acknowledged necessity, or what she called the 'inexorable law of consequences' and the 'undeviating law' of the world of science, she nevertheless insisted that our primary resource in the endeavor to flourish and live peaceably is the sympathetic imagination" (Gatens 2012, 82). Like Eliot, Smith reclaims those consigned to the margins of our attention and interest, and foregrounds them to remind us that those margins are thickly populated.

Indeed, "The Lazy River" is a celebration of the unglamorous – Smith turns our attention to the plexiglass hamster tunnels of our pricy resorts, the sun beaten plastic-packaged African tomatoes, the passive British holidaymakers in the lazy river goofing off, the worn and nimble fingers of the African hair braiders. Eliot's exhortation to a generously banal representation, so as to capture the world in its fullness, is consonant with her Spinozist ethics – it calls for the representation of the world *as it is*: replete with the labor and laborers who construct the world daily for its continued consumption. There is nothing less actually dramatic about the lives of people not considered worthy of protagonicity, for they are the centers of their own tales, and also consigned to support "our" bourgeois fantasies of self-sufficiency.[8] All of the things we cannot or will not do for ourselves – or desire others to do for us – exist in spite of our inability or refusal, and increasingly, capitalism's obscuring of them, to recognize them as integral to our being. As Moira Gatens remarks of Eliot's novels, they are a "self-conscious intervention into the way her readers imagine themselves, others, their cultural heritage and the present responsibilities. In short, it may be understood as cultural criticism" (Gatens 2007, 84). Novels are, in part, what help us to imagine what, who, and where we are in national time by virtue of the identifications we make, and the ones we refuse. Spinoza remarks on the mechanics of collective belonging, that is "if someone has been affected with joy or sadness by someone of a class, or nation, different from his own, and this joy or sadness is accompanied by the idea of that person as its cause, under the universal name of the class or nation, he will love or hate, not only the person, but everyone of the same class or nation" (Spinoza 1994, III.P46). In order to achieve greater understanding, we must understand first how identities, affiliations, and affinities inflect our interaffectivity. In identifying who we are, we must also seek to understand how we disidentify who "we" are, before we can claim to be ethical subjects at all.

Zadie Smith is cynically aware that under the conditions of twenty-first century neoliberalism and social media globalization, there may no longer be the incentive we once had to *be* good people. Tenuously immigrated Africans pick Spanish tomatoes for Britons, and for the most part, will never be seen or known to have done so, unless they have the social capital to make themselves known. "There is an urge to be good. To be seen to be good. To be seen," go the opening words of "Now, More Than Ever" (*Grand Union* 2019, 225). "More than ever," 'we' want to be perceived as good, but under that desire is merely the desire to be seen, to be distinguished from the mass(es), and worthy of being attended to without having to attend to others.

Smith's narrators are stumbling towards an awareness of the social-reproduction labor of the immiserated and often transnational or migrant (black) workers. In a similar moment in "Now, More Than Ever," the narrator narrates a viewing of *A Place in the Sun* by calling attention to "[Elizabeth] Taylor's parents' black maid [who] happens to be making lunch. You see her only three or four times, and she barely speaks, but let's just say that she had my full attention. . .Each time she appeared, I gave her a little improvised dialog, whispering it in Scout's ear: 'Yes, miss, I'll bring the dessert out now. I mean, my brother was lynched not long ago, down in Arkansas, but I can see you've got bigger fish to fry – I'll get right on it.' " (*Grand Union* 2019, 231). "Now" 's narrator performs the sympathetic self-projection that Eliot encourages, in a reparative reading that gives voice to the suppression of racial violence(s) that enable the world of the film. Race and class collude to background the maid, but art's incidental inclusion of her always-already gives us purchase to imagine her substance more substantially than the world depicted in the film does. In this way, too, we might look at historical/historicized/historicizable representations of social worlds with an eye to seeing the through-lines that continue to compose our present.

Smith's ethical push to expand the frame – of art, and of mind – to include and implicate the otherwise ignored subjects that co-compose our world *for us* is a kind of tonic to contemporary capitalism's fierce recategorization of the worker as a "laboring nomad" whose most recent tragedy is to be considered "superfluous humanity," "unable to be exploited at all" (Mbembe 2017, 3). If Smith locates this abjection in the bodies of African migrants, black British subjects, backup dancers and nannies and hairdressers, it is because "the term 'Black' was the product of a social and technological machine tightly linked to the emergence and globalization of capitalism" (Mbembe 2017, 6) and which Nancy Leong also describes as "racial capitalism." This latter formation is "the process of deriving social or economic value from the racial identity of another person" (Leong 2013, 2153) (*as in* slavery, but also its many derivatives) and which also describes the intercalation, historically, of race and class in capitalism's foundational slavery and colonialism's ongoing present. "The fierce colonial desire to divide and classify," Mbembe goes on to note, "to create hierarchies and produce difference, leaves behind wounds and scars" (2017, 7), which describes the earnest reparative work that Smith, and her narrators, are attempting in their ethical realism.

In "Fences: A Brexit Diary," Smith reflects on the changing dynamics of class membership – and identity-driven social memberships – and how the growing nationalistic retrenchments of the Trump-and-Brexit Era realpolitik *and* her own change in class status (she recalls she was once an inhabitant of a council flat, and is now the owner of a perfectly nice house) means that she no longer necessarily feels kinship where she once felt it. Wondering how to relate to others across the class divide, she remarks that it was once the case, projecting her I into a 'we', "we were all still willing to take the 'risk,' if 'risk' is the right word to describe entering into the lives of others, not merely in symbol but in reality" (*Feel Free* 2018, 28). Where once there was interclass encounters, a commitment to recognizing solidarities in spite of class, "in this new England it felt, to me at least, impossible. To her, too, I think. The gap between us has become too large" (28). The second decade of the twenty-first century has brought down the horizon on civil society, and growing inequalities, heightened fears, higher-stakes politics, have all conspired to militate against our mutual understanding. In our metaphorical lazy rivers, we circle and bypass each other, avoid engaging each other's gaze, and even if we wanted to, Smith muses, we just don't, preferring instead the material confirmations of fences or polytunnel walls (and Border Walls) as proof that our self-homogenizing social spaces are natural or nonnegotiable. After all, "When everyone's building a fence, isn't it a true fool who lives out in the open?" (*Feel Free* 2018, 31). The erstwhile-pragmatic narrator of "Embassy of Cambodia" justifies, "The fact is if we followed the history of every little country in this world – in its dramatic as well as its quiet times – we would have no space left in which to live our own lives or to apply ourselves to necessary tasks. . .Surely there is something to be said for drawing a circle around our attention and remaining within that circle" (23–24). There is a clear echo of Eliot's *Middlemarch* narrator and the warning against paying attention to the grass's growth and the squirrel's heartbeat. Brexit is, after all, precisely about asserting authority over to whom Britons belong, and by belonging, may be indebted to – and who they may, by virtue of redefining citizenships, include or exclude. But this is also an era when (natural, mineral, chemical) resources are actually diminishing, the climate is spiraling into catastrophe, and political instabilities are increasing. What happens when the question is not how long we can go round and round (our metaphorical lazy rivers), evading responsibility, but rather, what happens when we're no longer avoiding gazes, but peering into the abyss?

In "The Lazy River," a sinking suspicion slowly dawns on the narrator that their circular stasis is anything but natural: "Not everything goes round and round. Some things go up and--," before trailing off into a refusal to name the "down" that invokes the immanence and imminence of (climate; global) catastrophe. "One day [our children] will open a paper or a web page and read for themselves about the year – 2050 or so, according to the prophets – when the time will run out," and that hindsight will not save us from ourselves (32). What do we do on this side of that abyss? We are already immanently in it, and imminently in it – 2050 is going to come, whether we're here for it or not – and we aren't stopping it, either. How do we process the time to come that is inevitable from the time that has been? Smith's more recent narrators give us no good model, only the old faulty mirror of literary realism reflecting back to us the limitations of our interest in anything other than ourselves. If we fail, then, as Marcus remarks, "If nothing else, [Smith] reminds us just how lost we now are...[because] one of the ingenuities of *NW* is to capture this sense of immobility within the very structure of its narrative. This is a novel that lets out a lot of leash before tugging us back, before reminding us that we are not as free as we think we are." "Pock, smash" goes the badminton shuttlecock in "The Embassy of Cambodia," and the body of Fatou outside of its walls, pacing back and forth to the bus stop, as "we" watch her from "our" balconies. But our plasticity, Brilmyer argues from Eliot, means that we *can* change, be changed by narratives, and change others' narratives. This, in turn, may open up new axes for movement – up, and out; through, or over; instead of back-and-forth, or around-and-around. So, as Megan Watkins argues with regards to the pedagogical and eudaimonistic aspects of Spinoza's philosophy, every encounter contains within it the *affectio* and *affectus* – "the force of an affecting body and the impact it leaves on the one affected," a parsing that allows us to understand the breakdown of the work of education (Watkins 2010, 269). Our real and imaginative "inter-affectivity" helps us understand that the impact of our encounters leaves a kind of residue, affect that "accumulat[es] as *bodily* memory that...may evade consciousness altogether" (Watkins 2010, 277–279). Seeing the Other may not be part of the conscious composition of our consciousness or conscience, but becomes un-unseeable once seen, even with the mind's eye: the body thereafter knows what it knows.

The framework of austere realism – heir to the social realism of Eliot and Gaskell and other well-meaning nineteenth-century bourgeois writers – requires that we not exclude or preclude the othering subjects who labor to make the conditions of the world in which we pursue our own *conatus* whilst pretending that a vast 'they' doesn't exist. We cannot afford to be gormless, to stare agape at the Other in our midst without the attendant sense of fellow-feeling and fellowship with them. Zadie Smith is arguing that we cannot afford to be stupid, or if we cling to our stupidity we cannot but do so intentionally, inscribing circles around our attention that actively exclude the others we require. The African refugee or immigrant or migrant is always-already next to you whether you "see" them or not. Deepening this literary history, we might also seek to include the Spinoza of Mary Shelley in addition to the Spinoza of Zadie Smith and George Eliot, and what Eileen Hunt Botting articulates is Shelley's Spinozist "*apocatastasis*: a cyclical restoration of an ethical attitude of stewardship toward the whole world, with all its necessities" (1126). I see Smith's more recent work as an earnest attempt to articulate an ethos that may permit our survival in spite of our immanent end. We may be the gormless We on the balcony in "Embassy," and we do, and we must, *see* Fatou – but we must not let our gormlessness prevent us from acting ethically to support or augment Fatou's *conatus*, her striving to be in the world. Andrew helps her, after all, giving her a hand up and out of her ersatz-slavery; although he would undoubtedly justify that on the basis of common African identities; but "we" don't help her, we just gaze upon her, and "worried for her" (96). Smith's hopeful use of the word 'for' obviates other choices – "about" or "with," or "on her behalf," for instance – but it reminds us that the act of 'worrying' is a breed of passivity. Nevertheless, there is a small Spinozist space here for a greater ethicality that Gatens, poetically reading Spinoza, describes: "What draws us into sociability is our weakness rather than our strength, our tendency to imitate the affects of others rather than our independent judgement. We are querulous and opinionated – each wishing the other to follow his or her way of life, beliefs, loves and hates. . .Sociability is then a fragile union and initially, at least, be founded on imagination, fear and hope rather than reason" (2007, 81). "For" gets us closer to "with."

An ethical life consists in training 'our'selves – as the narrator of "The Lazy River" does, telegraphing the tension and difficulty of it through the terseness of the prose – to attend to the Other in their ubiquitous forms, in their commonest/common-ist presence. This labor is not a given, nor to be taken for granted, as it will require us to continuously interrogate our position and privilege, our affect and ethos, 'our' definitions of "us" and "them." It will not be easy, but it may be necessary for our collective survival (our *conatus*, our *apocatastasis*), and in the final line of Spinoza's *Ethics*, recognize that "all things excellent are as difficult as they are rare" (Spinoza 1994, V.P42).

Notes

1 Clare Carlisle's Princeton University Press publication (2020) of Eliot's translation of Spinoza (long overdue) promises to keep momentum in the discussion of the intersection of Eliot and Spinoza in the US and UK; Australian scholars, led by Moira

Gatens' long research, have marked out this intersection in publications, already, for the past two decades.

2 Lewes's *Biographical History of Philosophy* (1846) was one of the first overviews of Western philosophy that consciously included Spinoza, drawing a biography that lauds Spinoza's seriousness and dedication; "Bravery of the highest kind distinguished him through life, and it was not likely to fail him on quitting it; and yet beneath that calm, cold stoicism there was a childlike gaiety springing from a warm and sympathizing heart. His character was made up of generous simplicity and heroic forebearance" (393). As Matthew Stewart dramatizes in *The Courtier and the Heretic*, Spinoza's rational ethical philosophy was seen to be a challenge to the omnipotence and omniscience of (a Christian) God; and as Yirmiyahu Yovel explains, moreover, Spinoza was rejected by his synagogue for the sin of his ersatz-atheistic heresy.

3 Other critics, especially Moira Gatens and Dorothy Atkins, and Miriam Henson in her article "George Eliot's *Middlemarch* as a Translation of Spinoza's *Ethics*," spend much more time elucidating and articulating the finer points of Spinoza's philosophy, and any of these scholars' overviews of Spinoza will further spell out his philosophy for the curious reader.

4 It bears remarking that at least one critic denies this – or, at least, challenges the enthusiasm of literary critics for new readings of Eliot *with* Spinoza, arguing that those critics are "deeply mistaken," and that "far from being an epigone or appropriator of Spinoza, or even a fellow traveler with him, Eliot offers what is in effect a penetrating critique of his entire project" (Fay 2017, 119). Fay's critique rests on a distinction between Spinoza's idea, and Eliot's idea of sympathy, and although he never cites the article, D. Rae Greiner's excellent essay "Sympathy Time: Adam Smith, George Eliot, and the Realist Novel" makes similar claims without blasting Spinoza out of the critical waters.

5 Spinoza understands that the primary bi(o)polar orientation of our affects are along the axis of joy-sorrow, whereby joy is the "passion by which the mind passes to a greater perfection," and sorrow "that passion by which it passes to a lesser perfection," and this increase or decrease determines our capacity to be and act in the world (III.P1.S).

6 See also Beatriz Peréz Zapata, "An Endless Game: Neocolonial Injustice in Zadie Smith's *Embassy of Cambodia*".

7 Smith's use of the onomatopoeic "yelp" in this passage is sly and critical, as it invokes the contemporary customer review/complaint app Yelp, whose platform and algorithm expose the tenuous stability and success of any given service-oriented business.

8 See also Alex Woloch's *The One and the Many: Minor Characters and the Space of the Protagonist in the Novel.* We might also see Smith's evolution in conceptual protagonicity as a kind of rebuttal to the stylistic flattening that EM Forster describes in his *Aspects of the Novel*, which articulates that there are, simply, "round" and "flat" characters in fiction, without an attendance to the ideologies that impute that dimensionality to subjectivities. See, too, the emerging discourse of Social Reproduction Theory, which evolves socialist feminism to explain and account for the continuous production of our social realm for the smooth function of capitalism's division of labor.

Works Cited

Balibar, Etienne. *Race, Nation, Class: Ambiguous Identities*, New York, Verso, 2005.

Botting, Eileen Hunt. "Mary Shelley's 'Romantic Spinozism,'" *History of European Ideas* 45(8), 2019, pp. 1125–1142.

Brilmyer, S. Pearl. "Plasticity, Form, and the Matter of Character in *Middlemarch*," *Representations* 130(1), Spring 2015, pp. 60–83.

Eliot, George. *Middlemarch.* Ed. Rosemary Ashton, New York, Penguin, 1994.

———. *Adam Bede.* Ed. Margaret Reynolds, New York, Penguin, 2008.

———. *Spinoza's Ethics*, Tr. George Eliot, Ed. Clare Carlisle, New Jersey: Princeton University Press, 2019.

Fay, Brian. "What George Eliot of *Middlemarch* Could Have Taught Spinoza," *Philosophy and Literature* 41(1), April 2017, pp. 119–135.

Gaskell, Elizabeth. *Mary Barton*, Ed. Macdonald Daly, London: Penguin, 1996.

Gatens, Moira. "George Eliot's 'Incarnation of the Divine' in *Romola* and Benedict de Spinoza's 'Blessedness': A Double Reading," *George Eliot – George Henry Lewes Studies*, No. 52/53, 2007, pp. 76–92.

———. "Compelling Fictions: Spinoza and George Eliot on Imagination and Belief," *European Journal of Philosophy* 20(1), 2012, pp. 74–90.

———. "*Frankenstein,* Spinoza, and Exemplarity," *Textual Practice* 33(5), 2019, pp. 739–752.

Greiner, D. Rae. "Sympathy Time: Adam Smith, George Eliot, and the Realist Novel," *Narrative* 17(3), November 2009, pp. 291–311.

Henson, Miriam. "George Eliot's *Middlemarch* as a Translation of Spinoza's *Ethics*," *The George Eliot Review*, 40, 2009, pp. 18–26.

Houser, Tammy Ammiel. "The Ethics of Care in Zadie Smith's 'The Embassy of Cambodia,'" in *Critical Approaches to Literature: Moral*, Ed. Robert Evans, Pasadena: Salem Press, 2017, pp. 197–213.

Leong, Nancy. "Racial Capitalism," *Harvard Law Review*, 126(8), June 2013, pp. 2152–2226.

Lewes, George Henry. *Biographical History of Philosophy*, John W. Parker, 1857. Digital: https://archive.org/details/39002011211340.med.yale.edu/page/392/mode/2up, accessed: 3/5/20.

Marcus, David. "Post-Hysterics: Zadie Smith and the Fiction of Austerity." *Dissent Magazine*, Spring 2013, https://www.dissentmagazine.org/article/post-hysterics-zadie-smith-and-the-fiction-of-austerity.

Mbembe, Achille. *Critique of Black Reason*, Tr. Laurent Dubois, Duke University Press, 2017.

Smith, Zadie. *Changing My Mind.* New York, Penguin, 2009.

———. *The Embassy of Cambodia*, London, Hamish Hamilton, 2013.

———. *NW*, New York, Penguin, 2013.

———. *Feel Free*, New York, Penguin, 2018.

———. *Grand Union*, New York, Penguin, 2019.

Spinoza, Benedictus de. *Ethics*, Tr. Robert Curley, London: Penguin, 1994.

Stewart, Matthew. *The Courtier and the Heretic: Leibniz, Spinoza, and the Fate of God in the Modern World*, New York: WW Norton, 2007.

Uhlmann, Anthony. "Spinoza, Aesthetics, and Shelley's *Defense of Poetry*," *Textual Practice* 33(5), 2019, pp. 721–738.

Watkins, Megan. "Desiring Recognition, Accumulating Affect," in *The Affect Theory Reader*, Eds. Melissa Gregg and Gregory J. Seigworth, Durham, NC, Duke University Press, 2010, pp. 269–285.

Woloch, Alex. *The One Vs. The Many: Minor Characters and the Space of the Protagonist in the Novel*, New Jersey: Princeton University Press, 2003.

Zapata, Beatriz Peréz. "An Endless Game: Neocolonial Injustice in Zadie Smith's *Embassy of Cambodia*," in *Postcolonial Justice*, Eds. Bartels, Eckstein, Leiden: Waller & Wiemann, Brill/Rodopi, 2017, pp. 201–216.

3. *Transmodern Identity Construction in Later Zadie Smith*

Matthias Stephan

"Writing exists (for me) at the intersection of three precarious, uncertain elements:
language, the world and the self.
The first is never wholly mine;
the second I can only ever know in a partial sense;
the third is malleable and improvised response to the previous two."

(Foreword to *Feel Free*)

Zadie Smith is a prolific and challenging author, as her novels linger and make one question what one has consumed long after the reading has finished. This is one of the reasons that her debut novel, *White Teeth*, is still read and considered by scholars. Yet, Smith's work has evolved alongside, and along with, the times and her readers. The championing of cosmopolitanism by early critics has been challenged not only in recent scholarship on those early novels, but by Smith's later work as well. Multicultural identities are not as utopic as some would have us believe, but Smith's characters rarely settle so neatly into boxes; they are complex, defy expectations, and challenge notions of propriety, sense, and decorum. While that first novel arguably comes in the early wake of postmodernism, her later novels, novellas, and non-fictional works look past this mode to what follows – the complicated grounds of how to construct identity in a world without fixed structures, or at least with those structures underground and thus more difficult to see, critique or combat.

Academics from a variety of fields and national traditions have argued for a new vision of the future, one which has an optimistic outlook. This vision, articulated by scholars from philosophy, religious studies, politics, and literary studies, among others, (as noted below) promotes positive values such as sustainability, tolerance, and cooperation, and rejects those aspects of society that are deemed harmful or detrimental to sustainability, tolerance, and cooperation. This view is articulated as a "transmodern" position, a position which reacts to movements in modernism and postmodernism and proposes a way forward, a constructive, rather than a deconstructive, vision for humanity. A transmodern construction of identity, as I have argued elsewhere (Stephan 2020), is built upon the notions of postmodern identity (in which epistemological and ontological markers are eroded) to construct a new formation – however with acknowledgment that choices are constrained, not completely free. As Smith notes in *Feel Free*, "recognizing the reality of other people – and having them recognize the reality of you – is at the heart of the matter" (391) which can be articulated as a positive transcultural encounter, but also maps onto the construction of a transmodern identity.

I therefore use the notion of transmodernism, in its relationship to both postcolonial and multicultural expressions of identity, in order to address the question of how postmodern theory pervades contemporary literature, and how contemporary authors are reacting to that dynamic. Through an exploration of *NW, The Embassy of Cambodia,* and *Swing Time,* the essay considers how modernist constructions and postmodern frameworks shape how one understands the identities of characters, and then elucidates the formulation of a transmodern identity as a consequence of this intersection. The import of various class, racial and ethnic backgrounds, geographic migrations, and perspectives of the protagonists, all point towards a diversity of experiences that are not well articulated using modernist or postmodernist frameworks, or which they do not specifically address in their formulations. It consequently becomes pertinent whether a transmodernist identity construction produces a better model to understand our contemporary society.

The Transmodern Paradigm

The notion of the transmodern developed as a reaction to both modernist and postmodernist constructions in Latin America. The construction of modernism was heavily connected to the rise of colonialism and capitalism, and thus in Latin American thought, this is opposed to the organic and native understanding of social construction and consequently the ways individuals defined themselves vis-à-vis the governmental hierarchies and social norms. Postmodernism, differently than it developed in Western discourse (US and European), which accepted modernist frameworks which were built upon a Western centrism, develops in parallel with postcolonial critiques of Western imperialism. Thus, it is not surprising that Enrique Dussel, an early theorist of the transmodern, advocates for this paradigm as an alternative to the Western conception of the postmodern, as developed in other cultures outside of hegemonic Western discourse. In Ateljevic's words: "Dussel's (2009) central argument revolves around the role of intercultural dialogue in bringing about and defining the shift towards transmodernity" (Ateljevic 2013, 205). Through this appeal to the intercultural, Dussel provides a critique of the rise of modernist discourses, specifically the Eurocentric discourses he feels need to be transcended with the new paradigm. Dussel argues that the construction of the new transmodern paradigm needs to specifically include discrete cultural units that have been marginalized or dismissed by modernity (and postmodernity, in his view). This includes, in Dussel's reading, both nations and cultures of the Global South, as well as (in later formulations), within nations, disenfranchised cultural groups such as indigenous peoples. This would include, in many ways, the typical characters and landscape of Zadie Smith's works, from London to Africa. Dussel views the inclusion of these marginalized groups both as a righting of the wrong of exclusion, and as a way of infusing society with new (or other) ideas which can renew and move society, similar to the argument for multiculturalism at the time of *White Teeth*. In other words, his vision of transmodernity, especially in the construction of cultural identity, considers a dialogue between and among different world cultures, including those who have not had the chance to speak for themselves, and through which we, collectively, can develop a world-wide cultural paradigm. This inclusivity is laudable, but the formulation has theoretical problems.

Dussel's postulation derives from the deconstruction of global hegemonies, formed in postcolonial discourse and shaped by imperialist frames. His transmodernism champions an agency for previous marginalized areas, like Africa or specifically Latin America, yet, the critique, and its underlying assumptions, cannot be limited to creating regional or even national identities; rather, those arguments apply to further deconstructive manoeuvres to any overarching political structures. Postmodern scholars (in the Western sense) like bell hooks forcefully argue that we cannot try to maintain newly articulated cultural identities, like the African-American, or Dussel's Latin-American; rather:

> radical postmodernist practice, most powerfully conceptualized as a 'politics of difference,' should incorporate the voices of displaced, marginalized, exploited, and oppressed black people. [...] If radical postmodernist thinking is to have a transformative impact, then a critical break with the notion of 'authority' as 'mastery over' must not simply be a rhetorical device. It must be reflected in habits of being, including styles of writing as well as chosen subject matter. (hooks 1998, 626)

In so doing, in calling for theorists to practice what they preach, such a plea needs to allow for a complete deconstruction of discrete identity markers as culturally determined, and replace this with intercultural dialogue on an interpersonal and *ad hoc* consensual basis. Only through a politics of difference, where one's culture is not ascribed solely on ethnic, geographic, or national categories, can we allow the agency to articulate the transmodern conception outlined by Dussel, Rodríguez Magda, Ateljevic and others. This needs to be done by accepting the lessons of postmodernity, not dismissing them as politically charged, or as too closely associated with (articulations) of modernity.

Ziauddin Sardar (2004) articulates another critique of the essentialist notion of culture, which is that it allows for certain political and even religious groups to use positions of relative power to impose their versions of culture for political ends. By suggesting that national governments are not the correct group to identify the transmodern framework, Sardar essentially advocates for a more interpersonal solution. By eschewing "traditional" or "radical" versions of Middle Eastern governments, but entrusting the concepts to the people – presumably those that agree with him – Sardar moves us back from the identity politics traps of essentialism to the interpersonal. This appears in the later works of Zadie Smith, as her focus broadens away from NW London, and is particularly present in *The Embassy of Cambodia* and *Swing Time*.

If the position of the transmodern is to equally accept all viewpoints, to allow diverse opinions, then we need to open up the discussion beyond the essentialist views of cultures and transcend those divisive paradigms. Rodríguez Magda argues that we should read transmodernity as the synthesis of a dialectical process, not with the premodern, enchanted, society that Sardar considers, but with the modern and the postmodern. As she argues:

> "Trans" is not a miracle prefix, or the longing for an angelic multiculturalism; it is not a synthesis of modernity and premodernity, but of modernity and postmodernity. It constitutes, in the first place, the description of a globalized, rhizomatic, technologic society, developed from the first world, confronted with others, while at the same time it penetrates and assumes them; and secondly, it constitutes the effort to transcend this hyperreal, relativistic enclosure. (Rodríguez Magda 2017, n.p.)

With this formulation, Rodríguez Magda is arguing that transmodernity, as did its predecessor postmodernity (Stephan 2019, 74), functions using a rhizomatic structure, which not only acknowledges other cultures but subsumes them into this paradigm. She differentiates the postmodern and the transmodern, the latter not being based on the underlying model, but on its effects and its usage, as her argument presents the transcendent aspect of transmodernity with globalization.

The benefit of the postmodern era was the deconstruction of grand narratives that did not have epistemological foundation. This cannot, as she calls for, be replaced with simply a weak version of modernity: "Transmodernity prolongs, continues and transcends Modernity; it is the return, the copy, the survival of a weak, reduced, light Modernity" (2017, n.p.). Rather, I argue that it needs to be an assertive, reconstructive force in the wake of the postmodern condition. Accepting the legacy of postmodernity opens up the landscape for identifying epistemological frameworks upon which to build the type of society that transmodernity asserts is possible. This, I argue, can be done not through large-scale national efforts, but on a local level, and collectively built to a consensus on larger and larger scales.[1]

In the following sections, this chapter explores versions of transmodern identity in several of Zadie Smith's more contemporary works. This is done chronologically, as I argue there is an evolution to Smith's thoughts on identity and the presentations of its variety and perspective throughout her works. The chapter starts with the geographically labeled *NW* from 2012, in which there is a focus on characters who come from similar origins, in a variety of ways, but who have a diverse range of experiences. The chapter will then explore the immigrant experience in *The Embassy of Cambodia*, as reflected against a backdrop in Northwest London. Smith's 2016 novel, *Swing Time*, broadens the perspective again, with the unnamed protagonist traveling to both New York and Africa, and encountering other global citizens. Finally, the chapter ends with some thoughts from her essay collection *Feel Free*, integrating Smith's own reflections on her literary works. In each work, we see how the yearning to produce a self-narrative, a postmodern identity in the most assertively Butlerian sense, is tempered by external forces, whether internalized or directly met, and how that combination shapes one's identity, in a formulation I identify as transmodern.

NW

In the opening chapter of Smith's 2012 novel, *NW*, the character Leah picks out this line from the radio as important. "I am the sole author of the dictionary that defines me" (Smith 2012, 3). She tries to note this line down, while both evading the sun (which would wreak havoc with her pale white skin) and being fenced into her backyard, cut off both from the prying eyes of her neighbors (and thus protected) but simultaneously cut off from the perspectives and challenges of those around her. Her husband, as she recalls while lying in the hammock in their small, fenced-in garden, has noted to her that "not everyone can be invited to the party" (Smith 2012, 3). These contrasting notions, freedom to choose, and external constraints, set up a central conceit of *NW*, the construction of a transmodern, rather than a postmodern identity. In looking at a series of characters, with a focus on Leah Hanwell and Keisha (Natalie) Blake, I show how Smith has evolved in her presentation of her characters, moving from the 'Happy Multicultural Land' (Sommer 2003) to a more nuanced and difficult understanding of identity in the wake of postmodernism.

In many ways, childhood friend Leah and Keisha are very alike. They come from the same part of London, Smith's preferred setting of the North West part of the city, with the same experiences, schooling, attitudes, and outlook on life. Despite a brief period apart as teenagers, they ended up in similar situations by the time they reached college. "By July Leah Hanwell and Keisha Blake had been offered university places. Both had lovers. [...] Both the universities and the lovers were of an equal standard, despite their many differences. Both girls had grown into decent-looking women with no serious health or mental problems" (Smith 2012, 198). And yet, despite these similarities, and as the novel progresses and focalizes more on Keisha, now Natalie, Blake, we become both increasingly drawn into her own internal struggles with her identity, but also with the social constraints that she encounters – those that differ from both Leah's experiences and those of others from her own background. Natalie is more ambitious, driven, and achieves a level of economic and social success, and yet is dissatisfied with her life and meets a number of challenges based on external factors. Her story forms the bulk of the novel, and presents the framework by which identity can be approached.

Leah, while less driven by traditional social motivators, even those sought by her husband Michel, achieves a different level of happiness, or at least contentment. While Leah's story isn't foregrounded, and we aren't presented with the level of focalization to see Leah's internal motivations, we are left with an impression of an ease to Leah's existence, one which the novel contrasts with the struggles inherent in Natalie's trajectory. In contrast to those around her, Leah is presented as having more chances, despite similar circumstances. Her husband, of French African descent, for instance, connects their differences, "the many small differences in background, aspiration, education, ambition" they discover only once they are married, to her white privilege. "Of course, your skin is white, it's different, it's more easy, you've had good opportunities I didn't have" (Smith 2012, 29). That ease of existence, through no overt action of Leah's and despite her similar background with Keisha Blake (as well as Zadie Smith herself), is presented as problematic for the community, in how Leah is seen by others. "Although Leah has a blue tongue and a fancy degree and a hot husband and no offence, but for the women in our community, in the Afro-Caribbean community, no offence, but when we see one of our lot with someone like you it's a real issue. (Brighton weekend, team-building exercise, hotel bar, 2004). What kind of issue exactly was never made clear" (Smith 2012, 34). This differs in some respects from the reception of Archie in *White Teeth*. In that earlier novel, Archie's othering is put down to choices he has made, and "this strange way he had about him" (Smith 2000, *WT* 69) reflecting an internal sense of identity. For Leah, it is how she is seen by others that can be seen as problematic – her identity is altered by the perception from the outside. It is not, as postmodern theory would suggest, your 'inner' or even formal (education, relations, qualifications) characteristics that are ultimately at play, or completely define one, but additionally how one is perceived, and how that external perception influences one's own self-narrative.

This is further demonstrated in Michel's ambition to relocate to another, more suitable, suburb. Despite being viewed by his mother-in-law Pauline as suspect due to the color of his skin, and her association of "all of them, even if they are French, or Algerian, they are Nigerian, the whole of Africa being, for Pauline, essentially Nigeria, and the Nigerians wily" (Smith 2012, 16–7), Michel doesn't feel that he should reside in a 'Caribbean' neighborhood. His goal is to move "to another urban suburb more to his taste, which means more African, less Caribbean. To which Leah offers no comment" (Smith 2012, 90). In fact, one of the central premises of Zadie Smith's oeuvre is that your geographical origin is part of your identity, that coming from NW is different than coming from another part of London, and that one's social reality is predicated on one's neighborhood as well as one's neighbors.

Yet, the tale of Natalie Blake, which forms the bulk of the rest of the story, makes that geographical underpinning more difficult. Despite having the same geographical background as her childhood playmate, Natalie feels herself less grounded than Leah, most noticeably in Leah's absence. Up until this point, Leah serves Natalie as a ballast, providing her a means of identification – of which Natalie was unaware. Yet, "[i]n the absence of Leah – at school, on the streets, in Caldwell – Keisha Blake felt herself to be revealed and exposed. She had not noticed until the break that the state of 'being Leah Hanwell's friend' constituted a sort of passport, lending Keisha a protected form of access in most situations" (Smith 2012, 191). Without Leah's presence, and the context that this afforded Keisha's existence, she was at a loss. While this could represent a blank slate, the opening to the construction of an agential identity, for Keisha this was a source of anxiety – a loss of the grounding of her neighborhood, family, context. When visiting with Leah later, Leah claims that Keisha is "the only person I can be all of myself with," which causes Keisha, now Natalie, to confront "a fearful knowledge that if reversed the statement would be rendered practically meaningless, Ms. Blake having no self to be, not with Leah, or anyone" (Smith 2012, 208). In reaction to this, Natalie reinvents herself, changing her name, adopting new beliefs and philosophies, becoming intrigued by different aspects of culture.

> More prosaically, Natalie Blake was crazy busy with self-invention. She lost God so smoothly and painlessly she had to wonder what she'd ever meant by the word. She found politics and literature, music, cinema. 'Found' is not the right word. She put her faith in these things, and couldn't understand why – at exactly the moment she'd discovered them – her classmates seemed to be giving them up for dead. (Smith 2012, 209)

To a degree, this process of self-constructed narrative served her well. She succeeded in school, her ambition driving her to attain top scores and follow the career path – the law – that she desired. She met and married a man who was able to ease her life financially, completing two other typical social markers of success, especially for a woman, and especially for someone of Natalie's upbringing in a lower-class part of London. Smith wittily describes their relationship as "[l]ow-status person with intellectual capital but no surplus wealth seeks high-status person of substantial surplus wealth for enjoyment of mutual advantages, including longer life expectancy, better nutrition, fewer working hours and earlier retirement, among other benefits" (Smith 2012, 227) and this works to Natalie's benefit. She moves out (and up) from NW to larger, more luxurious, surroundings. Natalie has seemingly 'made it.'

However, this is not a typical *bildungsroman*, nor is the story of Natalie's identity that simply constructed. As Lynn Wells notes, Smith has constructed a multi-layered novel, and each of the sections adds to our understanding of Natalie's character. "While the 'guest' section thematizes the difficulty of recognizing the Other's true life narrative, the 'host' section enacts the role of the narrating Other while demonstrating its limitations, providing intimate insights into Natalie's thoughts and behavior while insisting on the fundamental unknowability of any person" (Wells 2013, 107). These two sides of Natalie's identity converge throughout the novel, playing off each other and sowing doubt into the construction of her identity. While it seems that Natalie has it all, she is deeply uncomfortable with her newfound life. She first encounters the type of bias built into her reception at the courthouse. While in school, Natalie felt herself able to achieve on merit, with few challenges to that perception. However, once she is in front of the judge in her legal role, she is increasingly questioned in her approach. Her colleagues, in particular white male colleagues, reflect the experiences of the judge; they "recognize each other. They are understood by each other" (Smith 2012, 239). In reaction, Natalie is advised by an older woman judge that she needs to present a different image, to change the external creation of who she is. She needs to ensure what is seen as "pure advocacy" by her colleagues is not seen as "aggressive hysteria" because her appearance is not "neutral" it is "never neutral" (Smith 2012, 239). This is seemingly Natalie's first lesson in needing to adopt an identity, in a professional setting, to be seen as how she sees herself. In this example, Natalie's intention and the new presentation are meant to coalesce into her inner and external identity matching.

However, later in the novel, as Natalie has an opportunity to join her brother at a party, she comes to realize that this mismatch between her self-perception and how others viewed her was ongoing. Her brother tells a story in which he boasts of both her confidence and her academic achievement. It may be that the story was simply intended to make her impressive to his friends, but Natalie takes it on its face, and in that light it challenges her own recollection of those events.

> Natalie did not recognize this story. She did not think these two things had happened, at least not in the same week, perhaps not even in the same year. She certainly did not get straight As. It had occurred several times this evening, these conflicting versions, and at first she had tried to tweak or challenge them, but now she leant back into the arms of a man called Paul and stroked his bicep. Did it matter what was true and what wasn't? (264)

While this could be interpreted as simply apathetic, in light of the circumstances, it presents Natalie's confrontation with other perceptions, and plays into her anxiety about her own self-narrative. Philip Tew, in discussing *On Beauty*, notes that "Smith's technique of overlaying and multiplying viewpoints, often refracted by others, is highly effective, adding depth to her perspectives" (Tew 2010, 102). This external refraction not only provides depth, as it has in Smith's earlier works, but Smith continues to use this technique to challenge notions of essentialized identities, and simplified internal narratives.

Furthermore, it was not simply the case that Natalie was ignorant of external perceptions and expectations, as the party anecdote could be interpreted. Further in that section, in discussing her pregnancy, we see her reflections on whether or not to conform to the perceived norms. "To behave in accordance with these images bored her. To deviate from them filled her with the old anxiety. She grew anxious that she was not anxious about the things you were meant to be anxious about. Her very equanimity made her anxious. It didn't seem to fit into the system of images" (Smith 2012, 269). Natalie's continued increased anxiety seemingly comes from her displacement from the NW, and her attempting to exist away from her roots. However, it is increasingly clear that external expectations fill her own self-narrative to a large extent. This challenges a Butlerian postmodern notion of identity, which is often associated with earlier Smith texts. The disintegration of Natalie's successful life and career, based on her self-destructive behavior is a product of this anxiety – a product of her not truly being able to self-narrativize as she attempted to do in college – but a lack of recognition that her identity is a transmodern identity, forged in the merging of an external pressure and an inner drive. Natalie discounted her NW roots, and that lack of grounding removed meaning from her attempts at creating a new self-narrative, especially as those choices she made were not made with an inner motivation which could anchor an identity.

Natalie's story comes to a head when she is confronted by her doppelganger in the form of Nathaniel, a childhood friend who did not have the opportunity to leave NW and leads a crime-filled life in their old neighborhood. Nathaniel's story, which we get in relief during other narratives in this complex novel, challenges the development of Natalie and the choices that she has made (including that of changing her name). He asserts that, based on their common background and childhood friendship, that he knows Natalie, and in his view, despite their now difference in education, wealth, and experiences, they are essentially the same. "I'm not a bad person, Keisha. Why you acting like I'm some kind of bad man. You remember me. You know who I am" (Smith 2012, 316). As Wells notes, viewing the characters based on reified identity markers risks erasing their inner narrative, the ineffable qualities. "[T]he characters in *NW*, with their secretive double lives, play dual roles as representations of certain aspects of the multicultural reality of contemporary urban Britain and as manifestations of the ethical danger of reducing others to essentialized identities based on race or other factors while denying their uniqueness" (Wells 2013, 99–100). Nathaniel's criminal nature is not explicitly presented by Smith, but enough evidence is presented, as Natalie/Keisha and Leah traverse nighttime NW with Nathaniel, that they determine they need to turn him in. Yet, even in that final resolution there is an understanding of the transmodern nature of identity. When Natalie, now once again Keisha, decides that they need to act it is based on their knowledge of Nathaniel's current identity, using his reputation and external markers, and not on his affective appeal to their childhood friendship, and his assertion that they know his inner self. He wants to determine that he is a 'good guy' in bad circumstances, but they factor in social expectations and legal parameters in making their determination. Nathaniel is more than how he wants to be perceived. Keisha's response to his appeal, as she states, "I don't know who you are. I don't know who anybody is" (Smith 2012, 316). In this she recognizes that identity is not fixed, and is an ever-changing relationship between self-narrative and context, especially influenced by the changes that context and circumstances have on one's self-narrative. Even the final line of the novel, with Keisha calling the police, reflects this split persona. '"I got something to tell you,' said Keisha Blake, disguising her voice with her voice" (Smith 2012, 333). The split between her voice (internal) and her voice (presented to the police) shows that her identity always changes with the audience, and that this forms her transmodern identity.

The Embassy of Cambodia

In 2013, Smith published the novella *The Embassy of Cambodia* in *The New Yorker.* The story focuses on an au pair, living in the house of a family in Smith's often used NW of London near the aforenamed Embassy. The story gives us another insight into life in the NW, and shows an expansion in perspectives in an ongoing development of her presentation of the identity of her characters. The story of Fatou, the hard-working African immigrant, allows for Smith to consider the position of those othered already from even the 'common' multicultural experience she describes in her earlier novels. As she does in *NW* with the introduction of immigrant spouses, she expands her attention by focalizing her story through Fatou, centralizing her story, the choices inherent in it, and the limitations on those choices provided by not only her socio-economic background, but simultaneously her gender, race, and immigrant status.

The transmodern nature of Fatou's identity is demonstrated by a series of anecdotes, which is how the format of Smith's story is created – it is presented as twenty-one sections each marked with the letter O. In the following, the chapter focuses on three aspects, the relationship of Fatou with her host family, her relationship with men (both in Africa and in London), and how she is viewed in the story by NW London itself (as seen in particular, by the narrator). This story, importantly, gives voice to the often unspoken even in Smith's narratives, and allows us to question who gets the right to self-narrativize and how the consideration of a transmodern identity, differently than postmodern identity, can allow us to explore the complexities of her perspective.

In the Derawal family, Fatou is not treated as an equal, she is distinctly not in the same social situation as her host family and she is made to understand that. This differs largely from Smith's earlier novels, in which there is a presented, even if challenged, solidarity of those belonging to NW. However, Fatou does not belong – she is not an immigrant in the vein of Samad Iqbal, nor does she acquire such a status through association, as does Clara Bowden. Fatou is a servant, and does not even feel free enough to leave (as her passport has been put away by her host family). As an au pair, she is provided a set of duties, but even as an employee, Fatou feels displaced, so much so that she 'borrows' from her employer (both time and access to the local health club) in order to find a way to escape and create a space for herself. In the end the family terminates their arrangement, not because she was caught stealing, or that she was doing a bad job, but because they needed to make room for someone more suitable. In this sense, no matter what Fatou's inner values were, her external characteristics and having the wrong background were all the Derawals ever seemed to need to know about her.

In an attempt to escape, Fatou latches onto a male friend, whom she meets through church. He is presented as nice and respectful, though not as attractive or particularly desired by Fatou. He represents, for her, security in the face of adversity and in light of her past. It is through Andrew that she becomes baptized, which represents for Fatou an ability to start anew, to reform her identity. "The day she finally became a Catholic, February 6, 2011, Andrew had taken her, hair still wet, to the Tunisian café and asked her how it felt. She was joyful! She said, 'I feel like a new person!'" (14). Through ascription to the Catholic faith, and its sin-clearing rituals, Fatou felt that she could wipe away her past experiences and recast herself.

This is a common immigrant notion, the need to create a new life and a new identity in a new country, but for Fatou this represents something deeper. Fatou had previously moved, with her father, from their homeland in the Ivory Coast to Ghana in the hopes of a better life. There she worked at a hotel, dutifully and in compliance with her own values and her father's expectations of her. However, not all of the clients respected her and one Russian businessman trapped her in a hotel room and raped her. The businessman assumed, afterwards, that she would report the incident and he would be punished, in line with his own expectations and social norms. However, the power imbalance between them, which Fatou recognized, indicated that there would be no consequence for this man as the hotel would not consider damaging the reputation of a valued paying client, and consequently she was presented as devalued, not worth challenging the norms for. Her inner identity was not important for him, and neither her status nor personal considerations would matter for the hotel. Fatou was not entitled to self-narrative. Not even her bodily integrity was hers alone. It was after this incident that her father arranged for her to be smuggled to the UK, where he hoped she would avoid such circumstances. The incident also changed how she felt about herself. In her eyes, as in the religion and likely her father's perception, she was now 'damaged' and a vital part of her identity – her virginity – had been removed. This was not seen by the rapist, nor is it clear from an external point of view, but through Smith's narration and focalization within Fatou, we understand that her seeking out baptism and purification by water was a means of changing the importance of this incident only as a part of her self-narrative. It becomes vital to the understanding of her character that this self-narrative is presented, but her own desires are not the only aspect as this incident provides a particularly harsh example of external factors altering a self-narrative.

This story is framed by the narrator's story, which adds a level of complexity to the creation of a transmodern identity. The opening of the story focuses on the walled-off Embassy, with its obscuring of a badminton match. The walls lead to the imagination of the residents about what happens beyond the walls, beyond the confines which they can see. Already here, one can see Smith pushing the boundaries of her created author-narrative, and introducing other, and othered, characters like Fatou. Beyond the wall, without the inner knowledge of what happens, everything is speculation – just as is the narrator's understanding of what goes on over the wall of the Embassy. "On the other side, a row of private residences, most of them belonging to wealthy Arabs (or so we, the people of Willesden, contend)" (*Embassy* 2013, 1). There is, of course, value in the stories of a local community, and one can extrapolate a lot about society through such a focalization. Smith mines the values and complexity of NW to great effect in all of her novels and short stories. This she draws to the reader's attention as well, stating, "Surely there is something to be said for drawing a circle around our attention and remaining within that circle. But how large should this circle be?" (*Embassy* 2013, 6). In this story, she pulls us to Africa and back, and explores the stories of those ousted from the multicultural nature of NW itself, as Fatou is forced to move in with Andrew.

Fatou leaving NW was the source of much speculation. As the narrator notes, "Many of us walked past her that afternoon, or spotted her as we rode the bus, or through the windscreens of our cars, or from our balconies. Naturally, we wondered what this girl was doing, sitting on damp pavement in the middle of the day" (*Embassy* 2013,19). Yet, much of this is due to lack of knowledge, about not learning about this underrepresented aspect of society (the underclass of the NW), but also presents a commentary on the nature of identity. External forces, as powerful as they are, are still not enough to know someone. The narrator, and the citizens of Willesden, do not really know Fatou, and we as readers only know snippets, fragments of her story, an incomplete rendering of her inner self-narrative, which needs to be tempered with our external view (and its impact on Fatou) to see her transmodern identity. This is true for other marginalized groups, as Smith explores in her short fiction, and in her 2016 novel *Swing Time* she then offers multiple viewpoints, beyond the multicultural mixing pot of the NW, as she expands her circle with each subsequent narrative.

Swing Time *(2016)*

In many ways, *Swing Time* parallels the construction of *NW*, with a focus on one of two childhood friends who grew up together in the Willesden area that often forms the focus on Smith's works. Yet, I argue that this novel represents another step towards presenting a more diversified perspective, in which the setting shifts from London (and therefore not exclusively NW), to include New York as well as West Africa, which allows Smith to expand her presentation of the identity formation of her protagonist and unnamed narrator. In the consideration of the transmodern identity, as the means to understand Smith's presentation, this section focuses on the narrator's identity construction, but puts this into context through consideration of several secondary characters: Tracey, her childhood friend; Aimee, her pop-star employer; Fernando, an employee in Aimee's West Africa charity; and Hawa and the villagers in West Africa. It considers how Smith uses the diverse circumstances and backgrounds, along with inner narratives and prejudices, to further demonstrate how identity formation can be seen as neither completely performative nor completely externally defined.

From her earliest childhood memories, the narrator of *Swing Time* described a life in which she was unaware of social factors that would influence how she was seen, and how she grew up with different circumstances than those of her peers, by virtue of her race. This can be seen through a pair of incidents, which are presented as instrumental in shaping her worldview, and through which Smith presents the factors that lead to the development of a transmodern identity. The novel's name derives from a 1932 film starring Fred Astaire, which features a sequence of Astaire performing in blackface. However, the narrator seems not to see the difference, despite it being "a film I know very well. I only watched it over and over as a child" (*ST* 3). Yet, after being reminded of the film as an adult, and seeking out a recording online, did she face the 'truth' about this performance.

> I hardly understood what we were looking at: Fred Astaire in black face. In the Royal Festival Hall I'd sat in the gods, without my glasses on, and the scene

> opens with Astaire in long shot. But none of this really explained how I'd managed to block the childhood image from my memory: the rolling eyes, the white gloves, the Bojangles grin. (4–5)

It is only upon reflection, now that she is older with a world of experience, that she is able to put the experience into a different context. It becomes not only a brilliant piece of dancing, one which she and her friend Tracey would watch to emulate Fred Astaire at his finest, but also, now, a demonstration of how her childhood self only saw part of the experience. Upon reflection, one understands that what one sees, one's own perspective, is not objective.

This naiveté by the narrator is contrasted with her friend Tracey. While the narrator has the idea that one can simply change one's surroundings, morph external factors to match how one feels inside, Tracey presents a grasp on how she is seen, and how things 'should be,' understood as reflective of social norms and expectations. For example, Tracey at an early age aspires to be a ballerina, as many young girls do. One incident recounts her drawing images of ballerinas, in which she demonstrates how ballerinas are 'supposed to look.' "I noticed that they were always blond, these plucky girls, with hair 'like silk' and big blue eyes. Once I tried to write 'brown eyes' and Tracey took the pen out of my hand and scratched it out" (*ST* 2016, 32). While the narrator, using a postmodern mindset, demonstrates a belief that one can be anything that you want, Tracey's image reflects (a childhood version) of the practical reality – there were no prima ballerinas that looked like Tracey or the narrator.

Tracey's eye for the practical also came into play in the schoolroom. She was the figure who grounded our narrator, forcing recognition of the structural racism at play. Despite the mixed nature of their upbringing, "half black, a quarter white, a quarter South Asian" and "[o]f the black half at least a third were half-caste, a minority nation within a nation" there was a distinct social hierarchy at play. It was Tracey who explained "[t]here could be no real friendship between Cabbage Patch and Garbage Pail, not right now, not in England" (*ST* 2016, 53), making reference to the series of toys which reflected a middle and lower class position. Despite these insistent lessons from Tracey, the narrator seems to remain blissfully innocent of the racial and social dynamics surrounding her. From her early employment at the media outlet YTV, to her subsequent hire as the personal assistant of the internationally famous Australian pop-star, Aimee, the narrator's experience seems to drift into situations without understanding. This seems designed by the author to present the reader these contexts in relief, allowing the reader to become aware of the social dynamics along with the naïve narrator.

The first such example is with Aimee, in an introductory session (in which they get stoned and get to know each other). Aimee suggests that she dislikes certain aspects of Britain, including the politeness and humor, associating particular stereotypical characteristics with national identity. When the narrator objects, distancing herself from the negative connotations and asserting a more independent identity, claiming, “I’m not that British,” Aimee replies, “Oh, babe, you’re as British as they come” (*ST* 2016, 108). This represents the disconnect between the self-narrative (the narrator’s own assessment of themselves as ‘not that British’) with external opinions (Aimee’s assertions that she is ‘as British as they come’). It also provides a split between national identity and local identity, as the narrator does not identify as British due to Aimee’s assertion of the stereotypical characteristics that entails, rather than other markers of identity, such as birthplace or nationality.

This is contrasted with Aimee’s own self-narrative and out-look on people. Firstly, she claims to see people via their individual characteristics, in a postmodern fashion. “[O]ne of my earliest lessons in her way of viewing the differences between people, which were never structural or economic but always essentially differences of personality” (*ST* 2016, 111). With this worldview, Aimee discounts social factors as instructive to an individual’s situation. This is convenient, in that she has achieved a lot, which provides fuel to her self-made image that she creates. At the same time, Aimee also views her own hometown as informative about how she thinks about the world. Aimee grew up with a working-class background in the Australian town of Bendigo, which contributes to her self-narrative even as she attempts to distance herself from the town physically. As the narrator presents, “[t]hough she’d left Bendigo behind – did not sound like her people any more, had always sung with a faux-American accent and often spoke of her childhood as some form of living death – she still considered her hometown a potent symbol, almost a form of bellwether” (*ST* 2016, 133). While it can be true that she dislikes and is intimately informed by her childhood, the presentation of Aimee as rooted by Bendigo is questioned by the narrator’s assessment of who she is now. This external assessment of Aimee’s character, which complements her image as an international pop-star and which seems to feed her actions more so than her heritage, forms as much if not more of Aimee’s identity than her roots. Rather than a disconnect between the self-narrative and external perception, this demonstrates the entangled nature of the transmodern identity, even if the individual is unaware of the dynamic in operation.

The racial aspect comes into starker focus when the narrative shifts to Africa. It is here that Zadie Smith pushes beyond her typical zone of multicultural spaces in Western identified areas, in which the dynamics of how identity is constructed plays on traditional postcolonial dynamics of a European nation with 'diversity' provided by cultural immigrants from non-European areas. *White Teeth* centers on characters with South Asian and Caribbean backgrounds, who have relocated to England, with their status still considered othered in terms of the English frame. *NW* and *The Embassy of Cambodia*, as discussed, have a similar trajectory, with the focus located in England. However, in *Swing Time*, we are presented a more sustained version of how 'Western' characters are interpreted by others, including West Africans and a Brazilian. In these interactions, the framing of characters as white, black, or othered changes based on the context, demonstrating that these categories are not fixed, and challenging Smith's normal framework in which she focuses on underrepresented aspects of English culture.

Starting with Aimee's Brazilian employee, Fernando (known as Fern), we see the benefit of his international perspective. In discussing the vast numbers of people in West Africa, each with a different NGO or charity and focusing on local issues, the narrator expresses dissatisfaction with the piecemeal approach, specifically referring to the interventions by white participants, including Fernando. In reaction, Fern responds: " 'These well-meaning white people. You think far too much about race – did anyone ever tell you this? But wait: to you I am white?' I was so startled by the question I started to laugh. Fern drew back: 'Well, it's interesting for me. In Brazil, we don't understand ourselves as white, you understand. At least my family does not. But you're laughing – this signifies yes, you think I am?' " (*ST* 2016, 251–2). The conversation is interesting, as in context Fernando thinks of himself as non-white, even though the narrator sees him as so. This is similar to her own experience, which she does not reflect upon. She is also viewed as black, in some contexts, and as not in others. She is referred to as black when hired at YTV, but is not considered as black in her childhood reflections with Tracey, who is darker than the mixed-race narrator. From an African perspective as well, the narrator is not seen as black, but rather as white similar to her Australian employer. After a dance performance in conjunction with Aimee's charity, her new friend Hawa, from the West African village where they are setting up the school, translates the villagers' response as: "Even though you are a white girl, you dance like you are a black!" which Hawa confirms with her personal opinion. "I say it's true: you and Aimee, both of you – you really dance like you are blacks" (*ST* 2016, 417). Aimee's reaction to this comment is one of amusement, and she takes it as a positive review of her dancing ability. However, for the narrator, it presents again a challenge to her self-identity. She is both seen as white, by virtue of her Englishness and skin color, but black in terms of her dancing ability, meaning race is also a category that is partly determined by external characteristics and is not simply a value of pigmentation. This is different from association of positive and negative characteristics with a racial identity, but moves towards a reconfiguration of racial identification based upon the social context.

By extending her perspective to encompass other worldviews, Smith challenges the Anglocentric presentation of her previous novels, expanding the impact of a transmodern consideration of identity in her later works. She takes this up further in her 2019 collection of short stories, *Grand Union*, which includes stories written before *Swing Time* as well as new stories which further this vein.

The Entanglements of Zadie Smith

The trajectory of Smith's writings reflects her evolving thoughts and experiences within and around London, New York, and her other travels. As she notes, the boundaries between her work and her self are themselves uncertain, which forms part of her only creative practice. "It's this self – whose boundaries are uncertain, whose language is never pure, whose world is in no way 'self-evident' – that I try to write from and to" (Foreward to *Feel Free* 2019). This chapter seeks to open up Smith's later work for this kind of analysis, and see how it speaks to the transmodern paradigm of our contemporary world. While it does not form part of the current analysis, Smith's own identity construction – demonstrated in her non-fiction collections *Changing My Mind* and *Feel Free*, provide fuel to the idea that her often unnamed narrators are an authorial insertion, which could be read as an onto-epistemological entanglement, in a Baradian sense.

Throughout the chapter, I have argued that the transmodern identity, which I describe Zadie Smith as presenting through the construction of her characters, is an entanglement of a postmodernist self-construction of internal identity, tempered by and in constant renegotiation with external factors which both frame externally and alter one's own self-narrative. Identity then becomes a matter of presentation, expectation, and a contested space of negotiation, rather than a fixed point or easily understood perspective. Smith's characters, as presented in the various novels, are increasingly challenged in their understandings of themselves, and their interaction with others. As Maeve Tynan argues, when discussing *On Beauty*, "Identity, then, is a matter of *positioning* as well as simply being. This understanding of identity as a journey to be navigated rather than a destination is central not only to Smith's own writing but also to her appreciation of Forster's work"

(Tynan 2008, 86). This journey is undertaken not just by her characters, but as Smith's oeuvre develops, her world expands and the development of the transmodern identity is further articulated, and more and more voices are included in the conversation. The narratorial voice presents an evolving presentation of the characters, both within each novel, and between them, allowing the reader to see this expansion. As the world increases its focus on the underlying assumptions our society has made, not least in the matter of race and gender presentations so prevalent in Smith's works, the descriptions of transmodern identities and how her characters come to understand themselves, however tentative and contingent, become ever more important. Smith moves the question of fitting into the immigrant experience, from the cosmopolitan descriptions of *White Teeth*, where everyone was displaced, to an examination of characters in her later works, with clear privilege in setting up their identity – showing the disadvantages of a purely PoMo postmodern form of identity expression, but also where the transmodern can provide a path forward.

Note

1 I am not alone in this assessment, as it is arguably also the position of Jeremy Rifkin in *The European Dream* (2004).

Works Cited

Ateljevic, Irena. "Visions of Transmodernity: A New Renaissance of our Human History?" *Integral Review* 9.2 (2013): 200–219. Print.

"Bold Type: A Conversation with Zadie Smith," *Random House*, February 25, 2005. www.randomhouse.com/boldtype/0700/smith/interview.html.

Dussel, Enrique. "World-system and 'Trans'-Modernity." *Nepantla: Views from South* 3.2 (2002): 221–44. Print.

———. "Transmodernity and Interculturality: An Interpretation from the Perspective of the Philosophy of Liberation." *Transmodernity: Journal of Peripheral Cultural Production of the Luso-Hispanic World* 1.3 (Spring 2012): 28–59. Print.

hooks, bell. "Postmodern Blackness." *Postmodern American Fiction: A Norton Anthology*. 1990. New York: Norton, 1998. 624–31. Print.

Rifkin, Jeremy. *The European Dream: How Europe's Vision of the Future is Quietly Eclipsing the American Dream*. London: Tarcher/Penguin, 2004. Print.

Rodríguez Magda, Rosa María. "Transmodernity: A New Paradigm." Trans. Jessica Aliaga Lavrijsen. *Transmodernity* 9 May 2017. Accessed on 04/12/2019 at: http://transmodern-theory.blogspot.it/. Web.

Sardar, Ziauddin. "Islam and the West in a Transmodern World." *Islam Online Archive* 18 August 2004. Accessed on 04/12/2019 at: http://www.islamonline.net/servlet/Satellite?c=Article_C&pagename=Zone-EnglishLiving_Shariah/LSELayout-&cid=1158658505216/. Web.

Smith, Zadie. *White Teeth*. London: Penguin, 2000. Print.

———. *NW.* London: Penguin, 2012. Print.

———. "The Embassy of Cambodia" *The New Yorker*. Feb 3 2013.

———. *Swingtime*. London: Penguin, 2016. Print.

———. *Feel Free: Essays*. London: Penguin, 2018. Print.

Sommer, Roy. "'Simple Survival' in 'Happy Multicultural Land'?: Diasporic Identities and Cultural Hybridity in the Contemporary British Novel." *Diaspora and Multiculturalism: Common Traditions and New Developments*. Ed. Monica Fludernik. Amsterdam: Rodopi, 2003. 149–81. Print

———. "From Transculturalism to Transmodernism: Representations of Identity in Zadie Smith's *White Teeth* and Chimamanda Ngozi Adichie's *Americanah*" *Transcending the Postmodern: The Singular Response of Literature to the Transmodern Paradigm*. Ed. by Susana Onega Jean and Jean-Michel Ganteau. London: Routledge, 2020. 109–132.

Tew, Philip. *Zadie Smith*. London: Palgrave McMillan, 2010. Print

Tynan, Maeve. ""Only Connect": Intertextuality and Identity in Zadie Smith's *On Beauty*." In *Zadie Smith: Critical Essays*. Ed. by Tracey Walters. Peter Lang, 2008. 73–89.

Wells, Lynn. "The Right to a Secret: Zadie Smith's *NW*" in *Reading Zadie Smith: The First Decade and Beyond*. Ed. by Philip Tew. London: Bloomsbury, 2013.

4. *"[U]nder the Sign of Love": Blackface Minstrelsy's Trauma, Racial Exploitation, and Kinaesthetic Hauntologies in Zadie Smith's* Swing Time

DR. ALBERTO FERNÁNDEZ CARBAJAL

In *The Lies that Bind: Rethinking Identity* (2018), Kwame Anthony Appiah establishes an important distinction between the antithetical ideas of culture posited by Matthew Arnold and Edward Burnett Tylor. After quoting Arnold's famous definition of culture as "the best which has been thought and said in the world" (Appiah 190), Appiah argues Tylor, an anthropologist, had a rounder understanding of it as "that complex whole which includes knowledge, beliefs, arts, morals, law, customs, and any other capabilities acquired by man as a member of society" (2018, 190). Appiah seemingly favors Tylor's less elitist understanding of culture, while, honoring his biracial heritage, he admits: "I begrudge nobody the things I also love, because, like Arnold, I can love what is best in anyone's traditions while sharing it gladly with others" (Appiah 2018, 207). Appiah's debate matches some of the dilemmas at work in Smith's latest novel, *Swing Time* (2016), where tensions are rehearsed between the innate fluidity of all cultures and issues of appropriation. Here, I propose a new way of approaching cultural identity in Smith's novel attending to the potentially troubling coexistence of de-essentialized cultural identities with art forms, such as "Black Dance", we are given to understand are inherited through a kinship perpetuating biological notions of race. These conflicting impulses in Smith's work between constructionism and essentialism are the symptoms of her mixed heritage and class guilt. From their bourgeois positions in the American academy, Appiah and Smith can reclaim a color-blind idea of culture that tokenises ethnic hybridity. *Swing Time*'s sharper counter-thesis suggests cultural relativism should not blind us to structural inequalities in our (neo)liberal democracies.

This article illustrates how Smith's deployment of white limelights and black shadows in *Swing Time* is complemented by the retracing of the peculiar genealogies of Black Dance. First, I explore the trauma of blackface minstrelsy, as well as the tension between timeless kinetic joy and the historical shame about the appropriation of Black Dance. Second, I explore what I denominate the ***kinaesthetic hauntologies*** of Black Dance in the text. While I suggest Smith's denouncement of black dancers' exploitation is progressive and her mapping of the hauntologies of Black Dance provocative, I conclude that Smith's sensibility is still too invested in the aesthetic standards of White Dance.

Swing Time provides both continuity and a departure for Smith. Like her previous novel, *NW* (2012), which centered on the close relationship between Leah Hanwell and Natalie/Keisha Blake, *Swing Time* similarly gravitates around strong female friendships, and relationships between women more generally. However, in this case, her main duo – Tracey and the novel's anonymous narrator – have comparable but not identical mixed-race backgrounds: the narrator's mother is black and her father is white, while Tracey's father is black and her mother is white. *Swing Time* is so far the only novel by Smith to have a first-person narrator. Nonetheless, this fictional autobiographical form does not lend the novel either immediacy or linearity. As Lindsay Gail Gibson observes, "[t]he narrator's *recherche* of her attachment to Tracey prompts the novel's temporal play. As if tracing the contours of an accordion fold, *Swing Time* zigzags between their 1980s childhood and the present day" (Gibson 2017, 138; original italics). This interplay between past and present and the ongoing haunting legacies of the personal and collective pasts has troubling undercurrents. According to Kaitlyn Greenidge, this is "the pattern of storytelling that one follows when one is relating a trauma – the eerie experience of the past as a continuous event" (Greenidge 2017, 197). The collective past of Black Dance and the characters' individual pasts haunt the novel's present. *Swing Time*'s focus on its protagonists' coming of age and its first-person narration recall Hanif Kureishi's *The Buddha of Suburbia* (1999), hailed by Smith as a formative text in *Feel Free* (2018). The close central female pair, sexual trauma, separation, a mother who creates a communal garden (however ill-fated), and the "return" to Africa, suggest the legacies of Alice Walker's *The Color Purple* and *In Search of Our Mothers' Gardens.* African American writing and Black British writing hence form part of Smith's transatlantic aesthetic inheritance, sensitive to issues of race relevant to both America and Britain.

Although at first glance it may seem *Swing Time* constitutes a paean to Smith's cinematic and literary favorites, the novel crystallizes into something else, a retelling of black dance history retracing Afro-diasporic spectral influences through the Middle Passage. Recent studies of Afro-diasporic dance have examined the proliferation of African rhythms and moves in the diaspora. Ananya Jahanara Kabir observes:

> it is these dances, variously termed as products of 'transculturation' and 'creolization,' which made African rhythms proliferate in diasporic space; these were the ur-forms of Latin social dances now enjoyed the world over, with North American dances such as the cakewalk forming an important intermediary step. (Kabir 2014, 113)

The triangular contact between Africa, the Caribbean, and America, creolized in contact with the music and moves brought by the European colonizers and slaveowners, gave birth to the rhythms and dances currently enjoyed the world over, and which connect black people across national borders and creeds.

The interconnectedness of Afro-diasporic dances derived from slavery and creolization drives me to use the term "Black Dance". Clare Craighead probes the concept, arguing that

> While Black Dance as a category of identification promotes (dance) work produced and performed by (dance) artists of colour, it also promotes a racist legacy which supports the dominant hegemonic discourse(s) operating within contemporary (global) society through the process of setting up an oppositional discourse of "the other". Black Dance as a category is by its very nature a category of other, because it politicises dance work made or performed by individuals of colour by implying that it exists within the racist superstructure of White Dance. (Craighead 2006, 20)

Craighead warns us that the notion of "Black Dance" perpetuates a racializing – and racist – vision of dance that constructs dance by people of color as always subservient to "White Dance", which is deemed to be either universal or the art-form's pinnacle. Despite the fact that the term "Black Dance" may be contentious, *Swing Time*'s investment in an aesthetics of kinship warrants the use of the term. Afro-diasporic moves are predicated as inalienable from black bodies, whether we believe this biological determinism is enabling or otherwise.

Containing black people within a paradigm of biological inheritance may indeed reinforce rather than challenge the problematic societal concept of race, yet Smith's depiction of the survival of black dance moves despite the gigantic historical odds against them remains provocative. Joseph L. Tucker Edmonds proposes that migration, colonialism, and theoretical creativity warrant an essential conceptualization of Blackness: "A genealogy of Blackness and a search for the ways in which cultures of Black-derived people have been shaped and moulded over time is a useful corrective, and the redefinition of Blackness, demand this. A genealogy of Blackness must address Atlantic and alternate diasporas" (Edmonds 2017, 213). I would argue that Smith's novel is invested in this idea of retracing the cultures of "Black-derived people" in order to redefine Blackness through the medium of dance as it travels in the Atlantic and postcolonial diasporas.

Smith's characters are affected by what I call the *kinaesthetic hauntologies* of Black Dance. In formulating the *kinaesthetic* – as opposed to the more common *kinesthetic* – I rely on linguistic and semantic assemblages. *Kinetic*, from ancient Greek, wraps the concept, suggesting an animation caused by an external factor, such as music. Embraced by the *kinetic*, we have an ancient Greek word and concept: *aesthetic*, which entails an engaged witnessing of art. Both phenomena are accented by one's *kin*, from Anglo-Saxon, linking movement and artistic appreciation to *kin*ship. I suggest kinaesthetic hauntologies involve a muscle memory of sorts, a combination of moves passed down aesthetically, through conscious artistic emulation, but also naturally, by virtue of instinctual physical reproduction, spectrally articulated, and often involving the belatedness and discontinuities peculiar to Black History. In a global order of hierarchical knowledges, Black Dance scholarship remains a recent development compared to the history of Western – i.e., White – Dance. According to *Swing Time*, the kinaesthetic bequests of Black Dance do not take place according to the logic of dominant Western knowledge, through the written historical record, but rather, in keeping with Jacques Derrida's work (1994), as a series of *hauntologies.*

"Hauntology", Colin Davis argues, "supplants its near-homonym ontology, replacing the priority of being and presence with the figure of the ghost as that which is neither present nor absent, neither dead nor alive" (Davis 2005, 373). The characters in *Swing Time* are haunted by the known and unknown black dancers of the past, who, mobilized via videotape, the internet, or through familiarly inherited moves, are neither present nor absent, neither living nor dead. Edyta Lorek-Jezińska and Katarzyna Więckowska argue that *hauntology* "and its variations have been deployed to account for a variety of tendencies and phenomena eluding more traditional and systematic approaches, running across disciplines and fields of inquiry. In this context hauntology calls for a radical reformulation of what constitutes the object of 'respectable' knowledge" (Lorek-Jezińska and Więckowska 2017, 16). In light of this, I would argue Tracey and *Swing Time*'s narrator push against the boundaries of what is considered "respectable" knowledge through their obsession with the neglected black dancers of Hollywood's past. In the narrator's case, this obsession with kinaesthetic detail enables the spectral retracing of a pattern of moves that emerges when comparing the work of current and past black dancers, providing a hauntological continuum of kinaesthetic inheritance.

Despite tracing such genealogies, Smith often eschews the task of describing dance in the novel in any detail, which could be either ascribed to her lack of specialized dance vocabulary or to her idea, explored in her non-fiction, that the artistry of dance is ultimately beyond language. In her essay "Dance Lessons for Writers", Smith asks: "What can an art of words take from the art that needs none? Yet I often think I've learned as much from watching dancers as I have from reading. Dance lessons for writers: lessons of position, attitude, rhythm and style, some of them obvious, some indirect." (2018, 136–137). These blatant and spectral lessons exceed language: they are articulated in the aesthetics of movement and rhythm – communal realities not easily translated into words that, similarly, may not be necessarily inherited through language. These kinaesthetic legacies proliferate in the interstices of the African diaspora. Black performance theorists Thomas F. DeFrantz and Anita Gonzalez offer a definition of diaspora involving issues of memory and embodiment: "Diaspora is continual; it is the unfolding of experience into a visual, aural, kinesthetic culture of performance. Like skin, it is porous and permeable, flexible and self-repairing, finely spun and fragile. And like skin on a body, diaspora palpably protects us. [. . .] [W]e wear memory on our bodies" (DeFrantz and Gonzalez 2014, 11). While linking white culture to intellectual pursuit and black culture to bodily praxis risks perpetuating racist colonial ideologies, the resilient communication of black performance is inspiring: it is remembered in the body, brittle – due to centuries' worth of oppression and repression – yet resilient; fluid and procedural, an ongoing combined process of manifest motion and spectral animation.

Swing Time is also fully aware of intersecting issues of racial inequality, cultural appropriation, and white supremacy. The white impersonation of blackness is central to the novel's articulation of cultural trauma. Love and theft, also the title of Eric Lott's book on blackface minstrelsy (1993), are key to Smith's cultural consciousness in *Swing Time*. The tense dialectic between love and theft is established early in the novel, involving an adult revisitation of a blocked-out childhood trauma:

> in the middle of the programme the director asked his interviewer to roll a clip from the movie *Swing Time*, a film I know very well, I only watched it over and over as a child. I sat up tall in my seat. [...] I felt a wonderful lightness in my body, a ridiculous happiness, it seemed to come from nowhere. [...] I felt I was losing track of my physical location, rising above my body, viewing life from a very distant point, hovering over it. [...] I hardly understood what we were looking at: Fred Astaire in black face. In the Royal Festival Hall, I'd sat in the gods, without glasses on, and the scene opens with Astaire in long shot. But none of this really explained how I'd managed to block the childhood image from my memory: the rolling eyes, the white gloves, the Bojangles grin. I felt very stupid, closed the laptop, and went to sleep. (3;4;5)

The narrator experiences a moment of artistic transcendence, in which her body and mind rise above her material circumstances, but such an episode of kinaesthetic joy is short-lived: her eyes and her conscience are forced to acknowledge Astaire's donning of blackface and his mimicry of black dancers in the eponymous film *Swing Time*. Her childhood self had blocked out Astaire's racial impersonation, a moment of trauma seemingly resulting in amnesia. Smith's text rehearses tensions between kinetic joy and cultural guilt, between timeless artistic pleasure and emergent historical shame.

Astaire's number in blackface has been interpreted as a homage to the black dancers Astaire learnt from in his youth, but this does not cancel out the political and material complications of blackface minstrelsy as an art-form, or his cultural appropriation of Black Dance for his own material advancement. Beth Genné asserts Astaire was "in 'awe' of the 'genius' (his words) of the African American dancers he saw in vaudeville and later on Broadway" (Genné 2018, 27). Such dancers included Bill "Bojangles" Robinson (1878–1949), whom Astaire met around 1915–16, when he was still a teenager.' (27) Astaire later paid tribute to Robinson in the number "Bojangles of Harlem" in George Steven's *Swing Time* (1936). However, Genné plays down the role of blackface in Astaire's performance, while highlighting his praise of the black dancers who taught him "steps between shows in the alleys outside the theaters" (27), kinaesthetic exchanges beyond one's kin and exceeding language that Astaire deployed to hone his dance sensibility. The "rhythm" tap that Astaire learnt from the African American dancer John W. Bubbles is also apparent in "Bojangles in Harlem". However, Astaire insisted on his own uniqueness. As Genné recalls, while influenced by Robinson and Bubbles, his dancing "was not the same. '*I am a creator*,' he insisted, and he was recognized as such by his early critics in New York and in London." (Genné 2018, 16; emphasis in original)

It is Astaire's prerogative, borne out of his white privilege, to pay tribute to Bojangles and Bubbles in blackface, but it is he who is in the limelight, and performing a genre known for its ideologically ambivalent yet materially exploitative relationship with blackness. Susan Gubar, in agreement with Lott, sees a complex dynamic at work in minstrelsy, "caught between a concurrent fear of and fascination with the black 'other'" (Gubar 234); yet this ambivalence cannot mask the fact that white performers were benefitting aesthetically and financially from the work of their black peers, whose fame and fortune never acquired the global reach or the stature of Astaire's.

What are we to call Astaire's unremunerated debt to African American dancers? Appiah advises that "we should resist the term 'cultural appropriation' as an indictment. All cultural practices and objects are mobile; they like to spread, and almost all are themselves creations of intermixture." (Appiah 208). Appiah's envisioning of color-blind cultural fluidity is favored by Smith herself in *Swing Time* and elsewhere. *Swing Time*'s narrator, who remains significantly nameless, is, perhaps like Smith herself, torn between the appreciation of the timelessness and cultural fluidity of dance and historical awareness about its unequal contexts of production. As she states early on in the novel, "to me a dancer was a man from nowhere, without parents or siblings, without a nation or people, without obligations of any kind, and this was exactly the quality I loved." (24) To the girl's mind, dance moves are owned by nobody in particular; they can be used regardless of location, ancestry, or nationality.

After her humanitarian stint in Africa, where her employer, the white pop star Aimee, manages to purloin an African husband and an African child, the narrator's adult self highlights issues of cultural appropriation:

> Earlier in the week, watching a costume fitting — in which Aimee, Jay and Kara were being dressed up to resemble Asante nobles — I'd hesitantly brought up the matter of appropriation. Judy groaned, Aimee looked at me and then down at her own ghost-pale pixie frame wrapped in so much vibrantly coloured cloth, and told me that she was an artist, and artists have to be allowed to love things, to touch them and to use them, because art is not appropriation, that was not the aim of art — the aim of art was love. (369–370)

Smith's white characters are vexed by what they perceive as the narrator's political correctness. Aimee defends her use of African dress by reaffirming color-blind ideas about culture. Aimee phrases her appropriation of African cultures as an issue of "love" belying issues of white socioeconomic supremacy. Her statement conceals the commodification of such love.

Curiously, Smith articulates a perspective comparable to Aimee's in her essay "Dance Lessons for Writers", in which she extolls that "[a]ll possible aesthetic expressions are available to all peoples – under the sign of love" (2018, 145). It would seem that Smith's character only partly agrees with Appiah's pronouncement that "I begrudge nobody the things I also love" (Appiah 2018, 207). Dance scholar Brenda Dixon urgently asks: "What conflicts arise when Black dance forms become public domain? Must the Black roots of a particular dance be reaffirmed publicly, even after that dance has become popular in the White world?" (Dixon 1990, 117). According to Smith herself, public reference is not altogether necessary but rather a more equal and ethical relationship with those subjects whose cultures affluent westerners imbibe. Smith celebrates the idea of cultural fluidity and the availability of all culture "under the sign of love", yet she does begrudge Aimee her unequal marriage to Lamin and her donning of Asante clothing. Aimee uses her white privilege to subject others materially, avoiding anything like rightful payment. It would seem that what is at stake here, in line with Appiah's thinking, is not so much "cultural appropriation" as racial "exploitation" (2018, 209).

The journey into adulthood of *Swing Time*'s narrator entails a recognition of this exploitation suffered by black dancers, yet there is an optimism in her conception of cultural hybridity that holds hope for Afro-diasporic kinaesthetics. Pondering on epistemic exclusivism, she inwardly confesses: "I knew there was something not quite right about [Tracey's] rigid notions – black music, white music – that there must be a world somewhere in which the two combined" (24–25). This creolized world, to her Hollywood-infused sensibility, is America, which she builds in her mind as the place ideally primed for the coming together of different kinaesthetics. But as the narrator discovers later:

> Too stoned in company once, I made the mistake of trying to explain what I found beautiful about the origins of tap dancing — the Irish crew and the African slaves, beating out time with their feet on the wooden decks of those ships, exchanging steps, creating a hybrid form — but Rakim, also stoned and in a cruel mood, stood up, rolled his eyes, stuck his lips out, shook his hands like a minstrel, and said: Oh massa, I's so happy on this here slave ship I be dancing for joy. Cut his eyes at me, sat back down. Our friends looked at the floor. The mortification was intense. (290)

In her role – similar to Smith's – of cultural historian, the narrator traces a kinaesthetic line, the hybrid inception of tap dance in its combination of the stepdance of Irish immigrants with the beats and moves of the Africans in the slave ships crossing the Atlantic. However, for Rakim, tap dance and minstrelsy are too politically fraught, due to their connection to the material conditions of slavery. *Swing Time* seems to suggest that cultures are fluid and malleable, that they create new art forms out of the coming together of different peoples; but it is also aware of structural inequalities, exploitation, and the capitalist commodification of culture.

The sidelining and obscurity of black dancers is best exemplified in the novel by the real dancer Jeni LeGon, who becomes Tracey and the narrator's idol: a talented tapper who was consigned to playing non-dancing maids, such as Ann Miller's maid Essie in *Easter Parade* (1948). Miller's tap number *Shaking the Blues Away* remains one of Hollywood's most celebrated dance scenes, while LeGon's tap routines in *Hooray for Love* (1935) and *Ali Baba Goes to Town* (1937) are obscure archival material for excavators of Black Dance history. Danya Tortorici asserts: "Following the narrator, we too can be mesmerized by clips of LeGon [...] and retrieve what risks being lost to the past. *Swing Time* is criticism set to fiction, like dance is set to music. One complements – and animates – the other" (Tortorici 2016, 34). LeGon is a catalyst of Black Dance history in the book. The narrator discovers her in a film starring Eddie Cantor – not coincidentally, a blackface performer, – *Ali Baba Goes to Town*, where the actress reminds the narrator of Tracey. Elated, she shows the film to her:

> All we had was her name, we found it in the credits. Jeni LeGon. We had no idea where she'd come from, if she was alive or dead [...]. And I had begun to spot LeGon here and there, bit parts in movies I'd seen many times. There she was [in *Easter Parade*] as a maid to Ann Miller, wrestling with a baby pug [...]. These discoveries [...] became a reason to call Tracey, and even if her mother answered Tracey would come round right away, with no hesitation or excuses. She sat inches from the television screen, ready to point out this or that moment of action or expression, an emotion passing over Jeni's face, a variation in one step or another, and interpreting everything she saw with that sharpness of insight I felt I lacked, that I considered, at this point, Tracey's possession alone. A gift for seeing that seemed to have its only outlet and expression here, in my living room, in front of my television, and which no teacher ever saw, and no exam ever managed to successfully register or even note, and of which, perhaps, these memories are the only true witness and record. (199–200)

Tracey and the narrator are haunted by LeGon: preserved in the postmodern medium of video tape, the dancer is neither alive nor dead, yet her moves are captured for posterity. Tracey zooms in on LeGon's kinaesthetics, compelled by her physical familiarity as a performer of color and by her joyful moves. LeGon's films become an alternative education for Tracey, key lessons in Black Dance removed from the classroom. Smith also foregrounds the spectral dimension of Afro-diasporic dance: the oblique yet resilient means of inheriting an aesthetics of black kinship.

In the absence of a dance floor, but in the presence of a magnetically inherited cypher displayed on a television screen, black bodies speak to each other in a recognizable kinaesthetics that ultimately exceeds language, remaining a "moment of action", "an expression", "an emotion", a "step": realities that

Smith herself cannot – or will not – find words to describe. Quoting dance anthropologist Judith Lynne Hanna, Halifu Osumare observes that "dance can be read as text, a nonverbal language with syntax containing 'an expressive form of thinking, sensing, feeling, and moving, which may reflect or influence both the individual and the society.' " (Osumare 2018, 6). These are non-verbal kinetic knowledges that exceed language; they transmit a resilient Black aesthetic despite slavery and historical amnesia, despite, even, time and place.

The novel's proof that white pedagogy is oblivious to the historical importance of Black Dance is the fact that Tracey gains access to dance education by becoming a copy of LeGon, an emulation that goes unnoticed by her white assessors and even her white mother:

> "The judges said they'd not seen anything like her [...] original *choreography*, not like that. That's how new it was. Never! I always told her that she'd have to be twice as good as the next girl to get anywhere," she said, hugging her Tracey into her mammoth blossom, "and now she is." She had a video of the audition to give us, which my mother took graciously enough. I found it under a pile of books in her bedroom and watched it alone one night. The song was "Swing is Here to Stay" and every movement, every blink, every nod, was Jeni LeGon's. (2016, 213; original italics)

LeGon's kinetic joy in *Ali Baba Goes to Town* is emulated by Tracey's "every movement, every blink, every nod," – elusively worded dance expressions. Despite the decades between LeGon and Tracey, Tracey herself remains unable to overcome the structural problems plaguing LeGon's career. As Hutchinson observes, "[f]ar from finding professional respect in Hollywood, LeGon was forever banished from the studio dining room, so to speak, even on *Easter Parade*", during whose shoot Fred Astaire failed to acknowledge her; "[i]n Smith's novel, this injury to LeGon is presented as a *trauma* not just to the actress herself, but in its full weight, as a blow to the young women of colour who follow her in dreaming of a career on screen" (Hutchinson para. 2017, 19; my emphasis). Ignored by her white peers, LeGon's film career eventually petered out. Tracey's own failed dance career becomes a traumatized spectral reenactment of LeGon's, still unable to overcome the sidelining of black artists in the entertainment industry.

If the teachers assessing Tracey's dance school audition are oblivious about Black Dance, *Swing Time*'s narrator becomes adept at tracing kinaesthetic lines. Her mother's interest in Black History, learnt through books, is paralleled in the narrator's pursuance of unwritten knowledge, chiefly the multifarious journeys of Black Dance. The main shadow dancer in the novel is Tracey's father, Louie, allegedly "one of Michael Jackson's backing dancers."

(36) He is a man "full of a kind of kinetic joy, but also somehow classic, elegant, Bojangles himself" (Smith 2016, 182). Louie stands in a kinaesthetic line, in the same continuum as Jackson and "Bojangles" Robinson. Although the narrator suspects the story about Louie's job has been concocted to justify his absence from the family home, she also observes the deeper historical truth articulated within it:

> Now see, with me, said Louie, [. . .] I didn't need dance school, matter of fact I used to rule the dance floor! This girl got it all from her daddy. Believe me: I can do all the moves! [. . .] [W]atching him I felt I understood now what Tracey had meant by placing her father and Michael Jackson in one reality, and I didn't find that she was a liar, exactly, or at least I felt that within the lie there was a deeper truth. They were both touched by the same inheritance. And if Louie's dancing happened not to be famous like Michael's, well, this was, to Tracey, only a kind of technicality — an accident of time and place — and now, thinking back on his dancing, writing it all down, I think she was exactly right. (Smith 2016, 186)

Smith's narrator highlights the alternative education provided by the dance floor and communicated kinaesthetically, from father to daughter, from black dancer to black dancer, in presence as well as absence. Even if Louie may not have really stood shoulder to shoulder with Jackson, he belongs in the same historical continuum, since they are both inheritors of Black Dance. This kinaesthetic hauntology, learnt and yet also seemingly immanent, constitutes a dialectic of private kinship and collective ownership, a resilient black aesthetic counteracting historical amnesia. As we will see now, the *aesthetic* dimension of the kinaesthetic is often overshadowed by ***kinship***, in a manner whose emphasis on the body may be ultimately too biocentric.

The narrator's humanitarian work in an unnamed African country completes her kinaesthetic fieldwork. Her foreignness and mixed heritage align her in her African hosts' minds with her white employer, Aimee; however, despite her racial misidentification, she completes her retracing of Afro-diasporic kinaesthetics:

> Eight drumming women later, [. . .] it was my turn. I had a mother pulling each arm, dragging me up. Aimee had extemporized, Granger had historicized moonwalk, the robot, the running man — but I still had no ideas about dance, only instincts. I watched them for a minute, the two women, as they danced with me, teasing me, and I listened carefully to the multiple beats, and knew that what they were doing I, too, could do. I stood between them and matched them step for step. The kids went crazy. There were so many voices screaming at me I stopped being able to hear the drums, and the only way I could carry on was to respond to the movements of the women themselves, who never lost the beat, who heard it through everything. [. . .]

> "Why are they saying 'too bad'? Was I that bad?"
>
> "No! You were so great! They are saying: *Toobab* [. . .]. So they are saying: 'Even though you are a white girl, you dance like you are black!' I say it's true: you and Aimee, both of you — you really dance like you are blacks." (Smith 2016, 417)

The narrator, whose flat feet have stopped her from learning White Dance (i.e., ballet), discards cerebral ideas about dance for the sake of making manifest her instinctual moves, in kinaesthetic communion with the African women on the dance floor, whose movements are attuned to the African beats. Despite the fact she is essentialized as white, she can perform African dance because it is part of her black inheritance – a blend of kinship and aesthetic which Aimee has had to learn and internalize but to which the narrator seemingly takes like fish to water. *Swing Time* suggests that, while Aimee's extemporization is informed by neocolonialist forms of human exploitation, the narrator's ease is due to the fact she is of black heritage: she carries this spectral kinaesthetic inheritance in her body.

Smith's character's plight chimes, to some extent, with Halifu Osumare's experiences recounted in her memoir *Dancing in Blackness*. Exploring her own journey to Africa after decades of studying and performing African and Afro-diasporic dance in America, she describes her dancing in Ghana:

> I was back in Christian Village at a funeral where the agbadza dance was again central. On this second occasion of the dance I ventured to join in the dancing to test what I had learned from C. K. Ladzekpo back at UC Berkeley. [. . .] Before I danced agbadza, I was this light-skinned, skinny [. . .], small-breasted woman [. . .]. But my dancing obliterated this perceived dissimilarity and brought me closer to the center of the village family. [. . .] Even though I knew the *movements* from studying with C. K., it was the music that I needed to understand more fully. [. . .] Before I knew it, a woman grabbed me by the arm and yanked me into the dance circle, facing the drummers at one end. The community clapped and sang, giving themselves more and more over to the spirit of the occasion. As I danced agbadza, the Christian villagers began to yell and scream at my execution, embracing me and giving me the thumbs-up. I felt that I had been preparing all my life for that moment — my first African dance in a traditional setting — and receiving the approval of the people from whom the dance came. (Osumare 2018, 177–8; original italics)

Like Smith's narrator, Osumare is conscious of being perceived as a racial and cultural outsider, but her moves propel her towards the African community. The two women are comparable because of their experience of African kinship through dance and its animation to the African drums. They are accepted as equals in an African setting because they can move in a way that is akin to that of their African hosts. However, unlike Smith's character, Osumare is well trained in African dance; also unlike Smith's heroine, Osumare is an accomplished and renowned dancer. Smith's text asks us to suspend disbelief in order to accept that someone like her narrator can pull off a feat such as Osumare's without any training. This poetic license reveals a biocentric sensibility that constitutes Smith's attempt at finding an essential blackness often denied to middle-class biracial subjects such as her character and herself. Nonetheless, Osumare's experience is hard-earned through aesthetic knowledge and practice, whereas Smith places much of her character's onus on kinship, thus potentially essentializing and fetishiszng the racialized black body.

Moreover, despite the fact *Swing Time* reclaims black dancers of the past while retracing the kinaesthetic hauntologies of Afro-diasporic dance, Smith's work remains continually focused on Fred Astaire. The narrator remembers

> a story about Fred Astaire himself once coming to Michael [Jackson's] house, coming as a kind of disciple, and he had begged Michael to teach him the moonwalk, and this makes sense to me, even now, for a great dancer has no time, no generation, he moves eternally through the world, so that any dancer in any age may recognise him. (Smith 2016, 38)

Here we have again the hopeful envisioning of dancers outside time and place; their eternal rootless and spectral existence. I argue that Jackson's enshrining takes place by mobilizing the figure of Astaire, the American dancer *par excellence.* Astaire may be – note Smith's tentativeness here – a "sort of disciple" to Jackson, but he has crucially set the standard for all dancers. Black Dance remains subservient to White Dance. This setting of a standard is perpetuated in Smith's "Dance Lessons for Writers", where the first dancer examined is Astaire himself. He is called "transcendent", and we are told that "[n]obody hopes or expects to dance like Astaire" (139). The essay ends with Smith's recounting of her meeting with Mikhail Baryshnikov, whom she asks whether he ever got to meet Astaire, to be told that the very movement of Astaire's hands was a dance lesson in itself (147). Despite Smith's best intentions, her work manages still to biologically essentialize the black body while culturally enshrining the white dancing body.

Swing Time is a novel haunted by the personal and collective traumas of Black Dance history: it traces a precarious genealogy of Black Dance and creates learning communities that challenge the epistemic biases of western dance pedagogy. Nonetheless, the world outside Tracey and the narrator's living rooms is not color blind, and Tracey's failed attempt at becoming a professional dancer, and the narrator's role as personal assistant to white pop star Aimee, remind us of structural problems assailing people of black heritage. However, Smith's original fascination with Hollywood films creates an epistemic bias: Fred Astaire, the main figure in the limelight, remains the gold standard by which every other dancer is judged, which means that white culture is not fully decentered. This is Smith's prerogative as a writer of mixed heritage who routinely celebrates hybridity: she can prize cultural fluidity and reframing cultural appropriation as merely so when it is an issue of financial exploitation, while still being epistemically driven to the dominant culture.

The promise of Afrofuturity articulated at the closing of *Swing Time* may be similarly linked to Smith's class privilege. Desperately advised by her regretful dying mother to adopt Tracey's children, the narrator approaches her childhood friend's block of flats, where she notices "[Tracey] was right above me, on her balcony, in a dressing gown and slippers, her hands in the air, turning, turning, her children around her, everybody dancing." (Smith 2016, 453) The novel seems to tell us that, despite the lack of literacy in Black Dance history of the Anglo-American cultural mainstreams and persistent issues of racial exploitation, the moves of the African diaspora are still kinaesthetically bequeathed; they are embodied by every move passed down by parents to their children, a kinaesthetic archive inherited through every means afforded by postmodern culture, in bodily presence as well as absence. This kinaesthetic blending seems to steel the legacies of Black Dance against the ravages of time and capitalism, creating bonds of community that, whilst materially fragile, remain seemingly impervious to the injustices of globalization.

Smith's qualified celebration of color-blind creolization and cultural relativism constitutes, nonetheless, a symptom of class privilege. Smith's dismissal of ongoing issues of cultural appropriation in her fiction and essays, despite the simultaneous consciousness of racial exploitation, belie an unwitting internalization of capitalist logic that is still complicit with neoliberalism. Smith's novel is a tale of Anglo-American capitalist individualism clothed as collectivism, and tempered by biological determinism: it tells the story of individuals who try to succeed in the cutthroat realm of show business, and it comes to the conclusion that, if you are of black heritage and working class, you will not make it. Smith's own personal trajectory suggests to me that *Swing Time*'s rebuke to the Blairite discourse of social mobility is a form of racial essentialism. Despite the fact *Swing Time*'s narrator is Smith's most autobiographically infused character to date, her socioeconomic trajectory – and let us not forget Tracey's – is dramatically different from her own. It may be that Smith would have arrived at more lucid answers to her questions about racial identity and social justice if she had considered more seriously the intersectionality of race and class in subjects such as herself. As an affluent cosmopolitan biracial writer, her literary portrayal of identity issues in *Swing Time* too gladly dispenses with an honest look in the mirror in terms of class, safely opting for denouncing what by now seem rather patent issues of structural racial inequality.

It is easy to see how a white character such as Aimee is exploitative: she uses her racial and class privilege for her own financial gain and treats other people and their cultures without due respect. What happens when a bourgeois writer of color like Smith indulges in abstract ideas of cultural hybridity, underscored by the obligatory cautionary tale that confirms her readers' awareness of racism? Then we forget that the love expressed in the arts indeed still means commodification; that some forms of creolization are no better than ahistorical conflation. A book such as Appiah's *The Lies that Bind* begins with a reference to George Eliot's *Middlemarch* and ends with a discussion of Constantine Cavafy and a quotation in Latin – mercifully translated – from Terence. While Appiah is almost certainly mobilizing the famous Roman playwright Terence because he was African and black – thus challenging an ethnocentric conception of canonical Roman culture as chiefly white – such knowledges of English Literature, modern Greek poetry, and classical Roman culture remain the remit of the still largely white cultural elite on both sides of the Atlantic. Comparably, an essay on dance by a Black British writer such as Smith begins and ends with Fred Astaire. When this happens so uncritically, we know that the notion of culture articulated by Matthew Arnold is being replicated by writers and thinkers of color and that the allure of white culture is still ongoing. Reclaiming the world's Jeni Legons while further enshrining the world's Fred Astaires leaves white culture uncentered and white supremacy ostensibly unchallenged. Given Smith's evasiveness in explicitly describing Black Dance, it may be time to discover new vocabularies that can cogently conjure up black cultures in a way that emancipates them from the enduring strictures of coloniality, not merely under the sign of love, but in the name of freedom.

Works Cited

Ali Baba Goes to Town. [Film] Twentieth Century Fox, 1937.

Appiah, Kwame Anthony. *The Lies that Bind: Rethinking Identity*. Profile Books, 2018.

Craighead, Clare. "'Black dance': Navigating the Politics of 'black' in Relation to 'the dance object' and the Body as Discourse". *Critical Arts: South-North Cultural and Media Studies*, vol. 20, no. 2, 2006, pp. 16–33.

Davis, Colin."Hauntology, Spectres and Phantoms." *French Studies*, vol. 59, no. 3, 2005, pp. 373–9.

DeFrantz, Thomas, and Anita Gonzalez, editors. *Black Performance Theory*. Duke UP, 2014.

Derrida, Jacques. *Specters of Marx: The State of the Debt, the Work of Mourning, and the New International.* Translated by P. Kamuf, Routledge, 1994.

Dixon, Brenda. "Black Dance and Dancers and the White Public: A Prolegomenon to Problems of Definition." *Black American Literature Forum,* vol. 24, no. 1, 1990, pp. 117-123.

Easter Parade. [Film] Metro Goldwyn Mayer, 1944.

Eliot, George. *Middlemarch.* Penguin, 1994.

Genné, Beth. *Dance Me a Song: Astaire, Balanchine, Kelly, and the American Film Musical.* Oxford U P, 2018.

Gibson, Lindsay."Kinetic Joy". *Dissent,* vol. 64, no. 1, 2017, pp. 137–41.

Greenidge, Kaitlyn."Shaken Out of Time: Black Bodies and Movement in Zadie Smith's *Swing Time.*" *Virginia Quarterly Review: A National Journal of Literature and Discussion,* vol. 93, no. 1, 2017, pp. 196–200.

Hutchinson, Pamela. "Hooray for Jeni LeGon: the Hollywood Pioneer Who "Danced Like a Boy"'. *British Film Institute.* 8 March 2017. https://www2.bfi.org.uk/news-opinion/sight-sound-magazine/features/jeni-legon-hollywood-dance-pioneer-swing-time. Accessed December 5, 2020.

Hooray for Hollywood. [Film] RKO Pictures, 1935.

Kabir, Ananya Jahanara. "Oceans, Cities, Islands: Sites and Routes of Afro-diasporic Rhythm Cultures". *Atlantic Studies,* vol. 11, no. 1, 2014, pp. 106–124.

Kureishi, Hanif. *The Buddha of Suburbia.* Faber and Faber, 1999.

Lorek-Jezińska, Edyta, and Katarzyna Więckowska."Applied Hauntologies: Spectral Crossings and Interdisciplinary Deconstructions". *Avant: Journal of Philosophical-Interdisciplinary Vanguard,* vol. 8, no. 2, 2017, pp. 15–24.

Lott, Eric. *Love and Theft: Blackface Minstrelsy and the American Working Class.* Oxford UP, 1995.

Osumare, Halifu. *Dancing in Blackness: A Memoir.* U P of Florida. 2018.

Smith, Zadie, *Feel Free: Essays.* Hamish Hamilton, 2018.

———. *NW.* Hamish Hamilton, 2012.

———. *Swing Time.* Hamish Hamilton, 2016.

Swing Time. [Film] RKO Pictures, 1936.

Tortorici, Dayna."Zadie Smith's Dance of Ambivalence." *Atlantic,* Dec. 2016, pp. 32–4.

Tucker Edmonds, Joseph L.,"Diasporic Dances: Theological Musings Betwixt and Between Blackness". *Black Theology,* vol. 15, no. 3, 2017, pp. 209–23.

Walker, Alice. *The Color Purple.* The Women's P, 1983.

———. *In Search of Our Mother's Gardens.* The Women's P, 1984.

5. *The Quest for Knowledge: The Intellectual Woman in Zadie Smith's Novels*

TRACEY L. WALTERS

Ten years ago, I wrote "Still mammies and Hoes," an article bemoaning Zadie Smith's failure to portray black women characters beyond the mammy, jezebel, and matriarch stereotypes (Walters 2008). These three denigrating misrepresentations of black womanhood perpetuated in the media are either contested by women who fight to disprove them, or accepted by individuals who internalize these false portrayals and develop a warped self-perception. In my article, I argued Smith's penchant for writing from the male perspective resulted in her inability to give an authentic voice to the black woman. Several years later, my view on Smith's characters has changed. Today, instead of stereotypes, I recognize countless examples of complex women standing in defiance of cultural norms and social attitudes about black womanhood. These black women characters fight back against the misrecognition of their personhood by seeking out alternative postfeminist versions of womanhood mirrored from their own real and imagined communities. These gynocentric communities affirm their potential to rise above the interconnecting oppressions of their race, class, and gender, which shackles them to their roles as wives and mothers.

My new appreciation for the black women characters in Smith's novels came after I detected a motif: many of Smith's black women characters are juxtaposed against male characters in various states of existential crisis: think Hortense and Archie, Alex-Li and Honey, or Samad and Alsana. While the male characters (mostly middle-aged) are dejected, infantilized, and impotent, the women are engaging in a process of self-examination leading them on a path toward a newly defined selfhood.

In the opening passage of *Their Eyes Were Watching God* (1937), Zora Neale Hurston observes the fundamental difference between men and women:

> ships at a distance have every man's wish on board. For some they come in with the tide. For others they sail forever on the horizon, never out of sight, never landing until the Watcher turns his eye away in resignation, his dreams mocked to death by Time. That is the life of men. Now, women forget all those things they don't want to remember, and remember everything they don't want to forget. The dream is the truth. Then they act and do things accordingly. (Hurston 1990, 1)

The women characters in Smith's novels, *On Beauty* (2005), *Swing Time* (2016), and the short story "Martha, Martha" (2005), are emblematic of the women Hurston writes about in the aforementioned statement. Martha Penk, Kiki Belsey, and the protagonist's unnamed mother in *Swing Time* are women acting on their desire to pursue dreams that lay dormant and unrealized. They are women who have always known (or come to the realization) that a life purely defined by motherhood or marriage is unfulfilling. Driven by social mobility, a thirst for knowledge, and a determination to reach their full potential, they renegotiate their familial priorities and venture out beyond the confines of the domestic to embark on intellectual journeys that redefine their identities as black women.

Education and intellectuals play a prominent role in Smith's novels. From *White Teeth* to *Swing Time*, she has created a plethora of erudite characters. Some are university trained, such as Malcolm and Joyce Chalfen or Howard Belsey and Mony Kipps, but others, Samad Iqbal and Alex-Li Tadem, are autodidacts in a lifelong pursuit of truth. Smith underscores the value of all kinds of knowledge, whether academic or experiential. There's a bohemian quality to the pursuit of knowledge for knowledge's sake. It's an exercise requiring time, and as Virginia Woolf famously declared, a room of one's own, and it is a luxury that was not always known to black women. Historically, in Britain and North America, black women had to fight for an education, and even when it was granted their knowledge was often undermined or challenged. In 1773, for example, before the African born poet, Phillis Wheatly, published *Poems on Various Subjects, Religious and Moral* (1773), she was forced to hold an audience with prominent men in Boston, Massachusetts to validate her authorship. Wheatley understood what scores of black men and women came to know. First, their knowledge would often be contested or undervalued, and second education was the tool for freedom and proof of their humanity. In America, black women had to wait until the nineteenth century before they could enter college and earn degrees. Ninteenth century African American feminist intellectual Anna Julia Cooper advocated for a woman's right to higher education. Cooper argued, "Intellectual development, with the self-reliance and capacity for earning a livelihood which it gives, renders woman less dependent on the marriage relation for physical support....Her horizon is extended. Her sympathies are broadened and deepened and multiplied" (Cooper 1998, 68–69). In 1906, Amy Ida Louise King was the first black woman (of Caribbean heritage) to graduate from Cambridge University. In America, Oberlin University was the first to open its door to women of all races. For the black women who matriculated, an education gave them dignity and purpose. After graduating they opened schools and became involved in their communities. Kabria Baumgartner explains, the quest for education for black women was about empowerment, and most importantly, purpose: "Purposeful womanhood gave African American girls and women the opportunity to study, to write, and to pursue knowledge – as activists, educators, community members, leaders, and, most of all, human beings" (Baumgartner 2019, 5). In *On Beauty*, *NW*, and *Swing Time*, Smith features black women who understand the power of education to transform their lives; but Smith is clear, the pursuit of knowledge is not always readily accessible.

The poet Audre Lorde surmised: women have "a dark place within, where hidden and growing our true spirit rises..." (Lorde 2013, 36). Lorde's articulation of the burrowed desires of women, especially black women, underscores the societal and cultural constraints obstructing the potentiality of women. The "true spirits" of women are often muted, shrouded by the veil of respectability politics dictating a woman's place within the family, community, and society. Many women are often socialized to suspend their own goals for the advancement of others. They are forced to accept the burden of parental responsibility or elder care, and as such, they are conditioned to prioritize family above all else. But there have always been women unwilling to accept social mores.

In 2019, lawyer Lara Bazelon made this point when she wrote an op-ed for the *New York Times* about prioritizing her job over certain aspects of parenting. Bazelon posited, "How do you excel at work and be the best mother you can be?" (Bazelon 2019). Her response was brazenly honest. "Every working mother gets this question which presupposes that a "work-life" balance is achievable, it's not. The term traps women in an endless cycle of shame and self-recrimination" (Bazelon 2019). Bazelon explained she chose to work long hours and missed her children's birthdays and school events because her work as a litigator was important to the individuals whose lives she was trying to save. Equally important were her own ambitions as a teacher, lawyer, and writer. She confessed that if she didn't fulfill her professional commitments, she would feel hollow. Bazelon courageously voiced what many women believe, but did not express publicly for fear of castigation. Bazelon's predicament of choosing work over family was due to time constraints, an issue Smith has addressed in her own writing. In 2013, she engaged in a public debate with a fellow artist/mother about productivity and the risks involved in having more than one child. Smith declared:

> The idea that motherhood is inherently somehow a threat to creativity is just absurd. What IS a threat to all women's freedoms is the issue of time, which is the same problem whether you are a writer, factory worker or nurse. We need decent public daycare services, partners who do their share, affordable childcare and/or a supportive community of friends and family. (Smith 2013)

Smith blames structural inequalities, gender norms, and limited support networks for the limitations on a woman's/mother's cultural production.

Regardless of the challenges of parenting and maintaining a career, Smith and Bazelon do not abdicate their parental responsibilities for personal agendas. In black literature and film there are few examples of women who withdraw from the pressures of marriage or the duty of motherhood. Black women's positionality as single mothers, othermothers, and pillars of the community, anchors their place in the domestic sphere. Typically, black women who leave their families are either fleeing from abuse, struggling with illness, or migrating for better financial opportunities to support their children. Notable exceptions are *The Color Purple's* Shug Avery who leaves her conservative home to become a blues singer and Camille Billops the protagonist of *Finding Christa*. Read alongside Smith's novels, *Finding Christa* serves as a useful case study for an interrogation of black female protagonists who, like Billops, make the decision to prioritize their own lives.

Finding Christa is a heart wrenching semi-autobiographical documentary based on Billops's decision to give up her daughter for adoption while she pursued an art career and traveled to Egypt for an adulterous affair with artist (and eventual husband), James Hatch. Twenty years later, mother and daughter reunite. The multimedia film co-directed by Billops and Hatch is constructed from oral interviews with Billops's family members, photographs, songs, journal entries, voice overs, and joint performances from Christa and Billops. The film has two main objectives: first it allows Billops to present her truth and explain why she put her daughter in care, and second it attempts to prove Christa benefitted from being raised by her adoptive parents. After Billops's fiancé abandons her at the altar, she refuses to accept that her gender renders her solely responsible for raising Christa. For Billops, motherhood was antithetical to the bohemian lifestyle she was beginning to explore. She needed the freedom to travel and work on her art, and Christa didn't fit within her agenda. Billops explains, even though she was unconscious of it at the time, she was tapping into a feminist ethos, "I didn't see this as feminist then. I just knew I had to reverse it. I wanted to be free of motherhood" (Billops 1991). In the film, Billops is unapologetic and insists her decision saved her life as well as Christa's, ultimately allowing them both to thrive. Christa has a different outlook. Although her adoptive family gave her a good life, she grieved her mother's absence. Ultimately, the film shows Billops was unwilling to sacrifice her own happiness at the expense of her daughter's well-being.

The altruistic nature of parenthood is a subject Smith has addressed in her own writing. Reflecting on the sacrifices made by her parents who gave up their lives for their children, Smith once wrote, "when I think of my parents it's often with some guilt: that I did the things they never got to do, and I did them on their own watch, using their time, as if they were themselves just that–time-keepers–and not separate people living out the ever shortening time of their own existence" (Smith 2018f, 362–363). Smith describes how her parents pursued their hobbies in snatches of time. Her father, an amateur photographer, used the bathroom as his dark room. Meanwhile, her mother used the bathroom as a make-shift greenhouse to remind her of her Jamaican roots. In the following works for discussion, Smith considers what it might look like if parents, specifically black women, chose to fulfill their own ambitions in spite of their children (and their husbands), and like Billops, put physical distance between themselves and their families. Smith presents three different scenarios to investigate this topic, each time creating mothers and wives who attempt to reinvent their lives and pursue their dreams on their own terms.

Martha Penk

How do two people from the same neighborhood take such divergent paths in life? This is a question Smith often interrogates. In "Martha Martha," Martha Penk is compared to her accomplished schoolmate, Kara. Kara has earned a law degree, purchased a large home, and moved up the social ladder. Beyond raising a son with her partner, Martha has done nothing remarkable with her own life. In *NW* (2012), Kara is reincarnated as Keisha Blake. Keisha is the first among her peers to "make it." Throughout the novel Keisha provides a roadmap for social mobility, but it comes at the expense of her identity, relationships, and sanity. Keisha's middle-class life is juxtaposed against Nathan Bogle's impoverishment. In school, Nathan was as intelligent as Keisha, but where she remains focused on school, he is drawn into a life of drug addiction and crime. *Swing Time* also investigates the alternative paths of neighborhood friends. In the story, after college the protagonist travels the world as an assistant to an international popstar. Alternatively, her best friend, Tracey, a talented tap dancer, has a brief stint as a professional dancer but ends up a single-mother of two living in the same public housing estate of her youth. In each case, education is presented as the fundamental difference between the characters. Smith doesn't suggest an education or successful career make for a more fulfilling life: Keisha is suicidal and self-loathing and the protagonist in *Swing Time* experiences her own life unraveling, but she demonstrates how it can offer a way out of poverty and the opportunity to improve the lives of the next generation. Smith often writes about social mobility. *On Beauty* (2005), an updated version of E. M. Forster's *Howards End*, centers on social mobility. In *Feel Free: Essays* (2018), Smith wrote about her own family's process of becoming lower-middle class. Vacations, spare bedrooms, and multiple bathrooms were indicators of the family's ascent "and represented, for my parents, a very British form of achievement. Raised in poverty, they were now officially what the census-takers call 'lower-middle-class'" (Smith 2018f, 355). When Smith graduated from Cambridge University and became a successful writer, she solidified the family's middle-class standing.

In *NW* and *Swing Time*, Nathan and Tracey accept the choices they made for their lives, oftentimes decisions that are driven by their poverty. As the mother in *Swing Time* posits, the cycle of poverty is difficult to break. "People are not poor because they've made bad choices...they make bad choices because they are poor" (Smith 2016, 49). In "Martha, Martha," Martha accepts the decisions she made as a young woman (chasing romance instead of an education), but after receiving a modest inheritance, she sets off on a path to experience life as it might have been if she had not started a family prematurely. Inspired by Kara's achievements, Martha leaves her son in England with his father and moves to an elite American college town to remake herself as a learned middle-class woman. In this fragmented novella, Smith suggests our futures are not bound by the decisions we make in our youth.

Martha's story takes place over the course of a day of apartment hunting accompanied by her realtor, Pam. As Lourdes Lopez-Ropero observes, consistent with many dyads in Smith's novels, in "Martha Martha" the "female figures are ideological opposites with divergent life trajectories" (Lopez-Ropero 2016, 128). Pam, an educated white divorcee and mother of two, shirks her own former materialistic middle-class leanings for a much simpler pedestrian life. Although she is the perfect guide to show Martha the ways of the middle class, Martha is uninterested in Pam, especially after learning

Pam left a stately home in an affluent neighborhood for a small house on the wrong side of town. The two spend the afternoon with Pam engaged in mindless banter, only to be met with Martha's disinterest. Martha's silences conceal what is known only to the protagonist – Martha has left her eighteen-month-year-old son at home to plan a new life in America.

Martha has one year to remake herself. First she tries mimicking the wardrobe of a middle-class woman, but from the narrator's perspective, she fails. Martha's "cheap-looking grey trouser suit and some fake pearls" are acknowledged by Pam, but Pam who is shabbily dressed herself does not stand in judgment (Smith 2005, 4). Martha's sartorial choices are just one part of a larger plan. Martha doesn't simply hope to appear middle-class, she also wants to adopt the language of the middle-class and possess the same cultural and intellectual knowledge. In addition to buying books, she seeks "to listen to more classical music. I want to know more about it. It's on my list." (Smith 2005, 7). Pam, a lover of classical and jazz music, is struck by Martha's business-like strategy to learning the music, which is antithetical to her own deep appreciation for the aesthetic and spiritual qualities of the artform. Pam admits to her limited knowledge of classical music: "I don't know anything at all. It's the violins that do it for me, I guess the way they sound like someone's crying?" (7). Pam is under the impression Martha is knowledgeable about music. She even asks if Martha is a student at the university. In this moment, Martha, who is flattered to have been considered on par with the college students, exposes her humble roots. She reveals college is a distant dream: "I'm looking for that next level – qualifications, getting forward, raising myself, my consciousness" (Smith 2005, 8). For Martha, at this point, raising her consciousness is more performative than substantive. Enrolling in college courses would be the practical solution for developing the critical thinking skills to help grasp a basic understanding of the subjects she wishes to learn, but her own intimidation, lack of preparedness, and limited finances results in her clumsy self-directed learning program. While there is something naive in Martha's chosen improvement plan, she believes it is the fastest way to change her life and experience some of Kara's success.

In Martha's words, Kara is an important role model because "she definitely took it to the next level – as a young black woman, you know? She didn't get caught up in – kids and that. She took it forward. That's where I'm aiming for – if you don't aim high, there's no point, really" (Smith 2005, 17). Martha's reference to Kara's race underscores the atypicality of Kara's accomplishment. Kara is the only black woman known by Martha to have entered the corporate world. Here Smith points to the interconnected inequalities hampering the social advancement of black working class women. It is also clear, Martha is raised in a community where higher education is the exception, not the rule. This is proven when she asks Pam if any black students attend the local prestigious university. When she makes the inquiry, she poses it as more of a fact than a question. Kara has exceeded the norm, but why hasn't Martha and others? Martha assumes it is because she put her energies in boys and other activities that distracted her from school, but poor decision making is not the main culprit for her working-class status, a factor that is beyond her control. While the narrator does not absolve Martha for lacking Kara's diligence, elsewhere, Smith addresses the correlation between social class and mobility. "To be born solidly middle class in England is still one of the safest bets in the world...a lot of the important chapters of a middle-class child's life story are already written; they are composed at birth. My children are very likely to go to university. They are very unlikely to become teenage parents" (Smith 2018f, 357–358). Martha fell into the trap of early parenthood, but fortunately, she is determined to evolve. She will not let her motherhood be the only thing to define her life. Moreover, Kara offers Martha an alternative image of womanhood; proof a black working-class girl can make it out of the housing estate and have a prestigious, lucrative career.

Martha is not content to live vicariously through Kara. Kara has inspired Martha to consider taking up law as well, but she fears her son will derail her ambitions. The trip to America has allotted Martha the time to invest in herself so she can be more than a mother. Initially, Martha believes she's strong enough to compartmentalize her duty to herself and her obligation to her family, so she asks Pam to look for apartments with a second bedroom and a garden, presumably for her son and partner. After visiting the apartment of a young intellectual couple, Martha changes her mind. Seeing the wife heavily pregnant with a toddler in tow, while the husband is in the kitchen, child free, alerts Martha to the trappings of motherhood. The couple also reminds Martha of her own family, and when the woman's toddler reaches out to touch Martha's face, she recoils. Martha's reaction paradoxically symbolizes both her rejection of motherhood and the acknowledgment she is missing her own child. When Martha takes a brief moment for herself in the bathroom, she produces a photograph of her son with her partner. Almost immediately she starts crying. On the back of the picture, a short rhyming verse from her partner pledges support for Martha's intellectual enrichment plan. The sophomoric poem betrays the partner's lack of refinement, which sharply contrasts with the new sophisticated life Martha is attempting to create.

At first, Martha's tears suggest guilt and a longing to reunite with her family, but moments later she is annoyed. The photograph reminds Martha of the responsibilities she has left in England, but (like Billlops) she refuses to feel guilty for her decisions. When she returns to the kitchen she instructs Pam to find a one-bedroom apartment, indicating her unwillingness to allow her emotions to derail her plans. Martha is a young woman at the beginning of her process of self-discovery and Smith leaves it to the reader to imagine her fate, but what would it look like if Martha was a much older woman trying to make up for lost time? *On Beauty's*, Kiki Belsey is well into her forties before she realizes she neglected the chance to explore any of her own interests. Just as Martha has Kara, Carlene Kipps is the motivating force behind Kiki's decision to reinvent herself and work toward a self-affirming life.

Kiki Belsey

Kiki lives the middle-class lifestyle Martha envisions: a large Victorian home, a solid career as a hospital administrator, and access to art and music. Whereas Martha would like to learn about culture, Kiki has spent her adult life relinquishing all things aesthetic or esoteric to her husband, Howard. Howard, an art historian, positions himself as the authority on culture, philosophy, politics and any other subject he deems worthy. He is a self-appointed cultural gatekeeper who regulates the Belsey household's consumption of art. Intellectually, Kiki lives comfortably in her husband's shadow, leaning on Howard's knowledge to the extent that after a while, she can no longer trust in her own opinions and loses her voice and identity. The outsourcing of Kiki's acuity is first demonstrated when the family attends a performance of Mozart's Requiem, a piece of music that brings Kiki to tears. Kiki enjoys the concert, but experiences a "curious anxiety" (Smith 2005b, 70). Unlike the white people who have an "enviable musical knowledge" (Smith 2005b, 70), she must rely on the program notes to comprehend the performance. Kiki attributes the white audience members' "enviable knowledge" to their race and perhaps their class, and cultural conditioning. Her deduction is not entirely true. In "Martha, Martha" Pam admits to Martha, she enjoys classical music, but she can barely comprehend its meaning. Pam is more concerned with how the music *feels* than how it should be interpreted. Kiki is proud that her black son can comprehend classical music. "*I* don't understand, she thought, but *he* does. A young black man of intelligence and sensibility, and *I* have raised him. After all, how many black men would even come to an event like this?" (Smith 2005b, 70). Kiki, however, is wrong to assume her son is unique. Moments later, another black male makes an appearance at the concert. Although Kiki does not understand the technical aspects of classical music, like Pam, she is spiritually moved by what she hears.

After the performance, Martha is excited to discuss Mozart with Howard, but he dismisses her enthusiasm, especially her assertion that they had listened to "the work of a genius" (72). Rather than accept her own opinion, she presses Howard to discuss the matter further, "because she was happiest when she could get him to talk to her about his ideas..." (72). Here, Kiki diminishes the value of her own intuitive knowledge and as usual relies on Howard's intellectualizing. What Kiki doesn't understand is beauty doesn't always have to be articulated. As her friend Carlene says, the beauty of music or poetry is that it can articulate what can't be uttered. Earlier in the novel, Kiki actually recognizes the limitations of her reliance on dianoetic reasoning. Watching her son agonizing over a letter to jilted his girlfriend the narrator observes, "Where Kiki had felt her way instinctively through her problem, Jerome had written his out in words....Not for the first time, Kiki felt grateful she was not an intellectual" (43). Kiki's ability to "feel her way through" her heartache, instead of her mind, underscores the value of her epistemological mode of thinking, or as black feminist Patricia Hill Collins says, alternative ways of knowing:

> This distinction between knowledge and wisdom, and the use of experience as the cutting edge dividing them, has been key to Black women's survival. In the context of intersecting oppressions, the distinction is essential. Knowledge without wisdom is adequate for the powerful, but wisdom is essential to the survival of the subordinate. (Collins 2000, 256–257)

The significance of this form of knowledge is reinforced by Kiki's friend Carlene. Carlene also emphasizes the gender distinctions between how men and women rationalize experience. Carlene argues, men move with their minds and women move with their bodies – meaning, men's actions are predicated on knowledge, but women's actions are motivated by feeling and emotion. Initially, Kiki disagrees and argues against the premise, but eventually she learns to appreciate both forms of knowledge.

Like many middle-aged women who mold themselves into someone else's image or invest in someone else's dreams, Kiki becomes a shell of her former self, both literally and figuratively. The curious girl who wanted to be a writer and aspired to be an assistant to Malcolm X, as well as a singer, never followed her own passions. Her dreams were repressed, first by her mother who wanted Kiki to pursue medicine or any other job that would provide security, and next by her children and husband. After spending her life raising three children and supporting her husband's career, she's stunned to learn he has been unfaithful. The affair prompts Kiki to reflect back on her life, and as she does she experiences what Jaques Lacan calls "méconnaissance," a misrecognition of the self. In her analysis of méconnaissance and its relationship to aging, Leni Marshall asserts, "Méconnaissance impels a person into a visual identity that most people consider to be less desirable than was their younger visage and that is less powerful socially, which can thus be considered an identity threat" (Marshall 2012, 58). As an aging black woman, Kiki is conscious of her invisibility and low social standing. While hosting a party, for example, she wonders how she's perceived by the guests: "Sometimes you get a flash of what you look like to other people. This one was unpleasant: a black woman in a headwrap, approaching with a bottle in one hand and a plate of food in the other, like a maid in an old movie" (Smith 2005 b, 98). As a black woman in a room full of mostly white academics, she regards herself as an Other, an archetypal mammy figure. Kiki's expanding bust and waistline further distort her self image. In fact, her voluminous breasts have taken over her body to the extent that once again, she is resigned to the same stereotype. She becomes what scholar Lisa Palmer calls a "split subject, a human being marked by a mythical assortment of telegraphic coding" (Palmer 2020, 512). Mapped onto Kiki's body is a catalogue of stereotypes attached to black womanhood: "sassy, sisterly, predatory, motherly, threatening, comforting – it was a mirror-world she had stepped into in her mid-forties, a strange fabulation of the person she believed she was. She could no longer be meek or shy. Her body directed her to a new personality" (47). Susan Fischer notes, Kiki's projections of these stereotypical images cause readers to pose "the same question Kiki asks at the beginning of the novel…'What am I looking at, exactly?'" (Fischer 2008, 111). After meeting Carlene and the Maîtresse Erzulie, she's able to answer the question.

Although they share only a few brief encounters, Carlene has a significant impact on Kiki and helps her to be introspective. On the surface, the two women couldn't be more different. In comparison to Kiki, Carlene is a homemaker and conservative Christian. Similar to Kiki, she's married to a pompous scholar who bloviates as much as Howard. Carlene, however, hasn't allowed her husband, Monty, to diminish her own efforts to enrich her mind. Despite these differences, the two women find common ground, and for Kiki, Carlene serves as a spiritual teacher/mentor. Carlene allows Kiki to express herself and indulge in discussions about poetry, art, and religion in a safe space where her ideas can be debated without being ridiculed or undermined. The more time they spend together, the more Kiki must admit to Howard's dominance and her own culpability in giving him control over her life (and mind).

Carlene is one of the few people to actually see Kiki as an individual, not a mother, a wife, or a mammy. Carlene has no preconceived notions about

Kiki. In fact, in their first exchange, Carlene asks Kiki if she's an intellectual. For Kiki, the question is profound: "And this was possibly the most important question Wellington had never honestly asked Kiki" (Smith 20005, 94). Why has Wellington not asked? Is it because they don't see the possibility, or perhaps because Howard is the known academic in the family. Furthermore, with her reliance on Howard, Kiki certainly hasn't allowed herself the opportunity to position herself as someone with anything to contribute to the intellectual community. Carlene asks the question because she has no reason to doubt this fellow black woman's capabilities.

Carlene does not describe herself as an intellectual, but she is well-read, speaks French, and is quite knowledgeable about art. Initially, when they try to engage in conversation, it's stilted. Unfortunately, Carlene's interests are incongruent to Kiki's. Kiki knows little about art and she no longer reads because she doesn't have time. Furthermore, she does not know the poetry Carlene references, and she feels as if Carlene is speaking another language. To emphasize this point, at one moment Carlene actually recites something in French, which Kiki can't translate. Regardless of these awkward exchanges, Carlene's probing questions instigate Kiki's metamorphosis.

When Carlene tells Kiki her son is getting married, Kiki thinks back to her younger self starting out life with Howard. In this moment "A clearing opened in her mind" (173) as she faces up to how much Howard controlled the thinking for both of them, how he created a curated version of their life together which "she let Howard reinvent, retouch" (174). Immediately after coming out of her reverie, she comes face to face with a portrait that was previously obstructed by Carlene who has left the room. Kiki is captivated by the image. The painting is of Maîtresse Erzulie, the voodoo goddess of love, beauty, and vengeance. In Erzulie, Kiki sees a mirror image of herself, a tall powerful, naked black woman in a red scarf, surrounded by flora and fauna, a symbolic figure of death and rebirth. Erzulie, bourne out of an alternative Caribbean conception of black womanhood, is juxtaposed against the stereotypical mammy, the configuration of white supremacist ideology. Due to Howard's prohibition of portraits in the home, Kiki is unfamiliar with the Hyppolite painting. Carlene notices Kiki's admiration and educates her about the goddess and her powers, explaining Erzulie represents "the ideal female" (175). The statement and the portrait leave an indelible impression on Kiki who wants to behold some of the goddess's characteristics, especially vengeance. With Carlene and Erzulie, for the first time, Kiki finds a woman who validates her existence.

During her time with Kiki, Carlene is given permission to be vulnerable. She opens up about her past and her aspirations. What's most revealing is her interest in living an alternative lifestyle with a woman, an aspiration she didn't have the courage to follow-through with in her younger years. Carlene holds no judgment. Kiki also admits to struggling in her marriage and the choices she's made for her life. She tells Carlene, "Right now I'm trying to understand what my life's been *for*—" (Smith 2005, 176). Conversely, Carlene says she thinks of her own life from the position "*who* has my life been for?" Kiki pushes back against the statement. In her life, the "who" is Howard, but at this juncture, her focus is on her personal legacy. She's not yet able to define the purpose or meaning of her life.

After several meetings with Carlene, Kiki has a reawakening. She finally admits Howard is a fraud, a weak, fearful man reliant on rhetoric and bombast, and not the great man she conjured in her mind. Howard is so busy performing as an intellect he can't face the real world. Victoria Arana notes, all the rhetoric and pontificating in the novel "show[s] how very infrequently a publicly espoused ideology bears any relationship to the individual's daily life" (Arana 2012). Finally, Kiki recognizes how much she's intellectually stunted and decides to abandon Howard's beliefs. She starts by debating with Monty Kipps, Carlene's husband and Howard's nemesis. Monty's radical views on Affirmative Action have long been dismissed in the Belsey home, but Kiki has never been given license to discuss the issue with anyone besides Howard. When she's presented with an opportunity to engage in a spirited argument with Monty himself, she does so without faltering or depending on Howard's rhetoric. Following her conversation with Monty, she is intrigued to learn more and attends one of his lectures. It's a treasonous act, but Kiki resolves that Howard is no longer the priority or the authority. Unsurprisingly, when Howard discovers Kiki attended the meeting he is outraged. The recognition that he has lost his ability to dominate Kiki bruises his ego. Kiki chastises Howard for being "like the thought police" (393) and makes a case for "trying to get all points of view" (392). Howard refuses to hear Kiki, but she is resolute: "I'm still *in* here. And I don't want to be *resented* or *despised* for changing...I'd rather be alone" (398).

In order to be truly free and independent, Kiki must live on her own terms without judgment and with the openness to receive new experiences. Without warning, she leaves Howard and the children and moves in with a friend, who is much to Howard's chagrin a lesbian. It's not stated that the two are in a relationship, but from earlier statements, it's clear if there is mutual interest, Kiki is open to the possibility of exploring something new. More importantly, she demonstrates she is acting from emotion rather than thought. Kiki's departure comes at the brink of Howard's unraveling. Howard is up for tenure and preparing to give a lecture that will determine the fate of his career. Howard resents Kiki's liberation and he is equally threatened by her roommate, but he can do nothing to save his marriage. In the end, Kiki enjoys her freedom and the opportunity to rediscover herself and her voice as she searches for the true meaning of her life. Whereas Kiki has to wait until she is a woman in her prime before she can gain control of her life, the mother in *Swing Time* decides early on whom she lives for and what she lives for. The answer is clear. She has created a life that advances herself as a woman, her daughter, and eventually her community.

The Mother

In *Swing Time*, the mother figure is fully transformed into a confident, ambitious woman. Where Martha finds inspiration from Kara and Kiki draws strength from Erzulie and Carlene, in this work, the mother's self-affirming figures of black womanhood are found outside the immediate community. Here, the mother identifies with western feminist sheroes of the 1980s, such as Angela Davis and Gloria Steinem. The mother is portrayed from the perspective of the protagonist who is looking back over her own life. The protagonist describes her mother as a feminist, "one with a vision to shake the world like Angela Davis, a woman driving toward 'the higher concepts'" (Smith 2016, 10). Women like Davis propagate the mantras of female liberation that drive her mother to take Martha's approach to motherhood as she unapologetically pours herself into her career. In *Of Woman Born: Motherhood as Experience and Institution*, feminst critic Adrienne Rich argued there are "two meanings of motherhood, one superimposed on the other: the *potential* relationship of any woman to her powers or reproduction – and to the children; and the institution – which aims at ensuring that that potential – and all women – shall remain under male control" (Rich 1977, 13). The mother in *Swing Time* acknowledges this difference between motherhood as an institution versus "mothering" as a chosen maternal experience.

From the onset, the novel's protagonist perceives her mother as "a woman plotting her escape, from me, from the very role of motherhood" (Smith 18). Thus, she rejects all restrictions on her womanhood and makes her husband primary caretaker of the home, even though she's not the breadwinner – what she brings into the home is intellectual currency. This mother has the same middle-class aspirations as Martha, but not the barriers. She married early, but she refuses to conform and be like the other women in her community – doting mothers living vicariously through their children's dreams of becoming dancers and singers. The women are the inverse of mirrored images that can affirm her womanhood. Similar to the other texts referenced in this essay, the mother is given her own foil, the protagonist's best friend's mother. This woman is from the same housing estate, but their mentalities and circumstances are different. She is neither educated or ambitious and her life revolves around her daughter. The narrator says although her mother cared about the women in her community, she saw herself as different. Unlike these other women, she's focused on her own ascent, as well as her daughter's. Most community women seem content, but she is working hard on her self-improvement plan and strategy to attain middle-class status, which she performs through the accent she uses on the phone and the attire she acquires at garden sales (a more successful version of the sartorial passing attempted by Martha). Her performance constructs an imagined version of self, quite antithetical to how Kiki viewed herself. She has the courage to write her own rules and refuses to adhere to gender norms.

While other mothers congregate in school yards and ballet practice and recitals, she prefers to read, not simply novels, but esoteric work, philosophy and history. The narrator, not yet a teen, has no appreciation and laments:

> My own mother's focus was always elsewhere. She could never simply sit somewhere and let the time pass, she had to be learning something. She might arrive at the beginning of class with, say, *The Black Jacobins* in hand, and by the time I came over to ask her to swap my ballet shoes for tap she would already be a hundred pages through. (Smith 2016, 16)

Her mother's disinterest in ballet lessons mirrors her dismissal of the gendered rearing of girls. While this mother entertains her daughter's penchant for dance as an important social activity, she finds the activity "frivolous," and forces her husband to bring their daughter to class – again underscoring her abdication of her assigned gender role. The mother is not totally against creative expression. On a whim, she decides to create a communal vegetable/flower garden, but when she discovers there is more clay than soil, she conducts an impromptu pottery class for the neighborhood children. From the protagonist's perspective, the mother's exercise is as much about creativity as it is about the exhibition of a "new concept in parenting" being demonstrated on their balcony.

> She was essentially asking the whole estate a question. What if we didn't plonk our children in front of the telly each day, to watch cartoons and soap operas? What if we gave them, instead, a lump of clay, and poured water over it, and showed them how to spin it round until a shape formed between their hands? What kind of society would that be? (Smith 2016, 61)

Consistent with her ethos, the mother privileges the nurturing of intellect. Teaching her daughter, and playmates, to use one's imagination is the kind of parenting she finds meaningful and productive. After all, she muses, any of them could become the next Augusta Savage, the famed African American woman sculptor. Although later in life the narrator appreciates her mother's alternative model of parenting, at the time, she wishes her mother could be more available. She laments, "I couldn't get her complete submission" (Smith 2016, 18) and neither could her father.

The protagonist's father is a shell of a man, forced to accept his emasculation. Not only is he mother and father to his daughter, he has also lost the battle to prove his virility. The mother recognizes what an expanded family means for her own future, and determined to hold on to her independence, she refuses to bear a second child. Unlike Kiki who relies on Howard for knowledge, in *Swing Time* the roles are reversed; it's the father who can't understand his wife. The mother evolves intellectually and outgrows her husband. In a sense, she becomes like Howard, speaking another language, unintelligible to her husband and daughter to the extent she "had to keep explaining her terms" (Smith 2016, 35). While the husband tries reading *The Communist Manifesto*, which he affectionately calls his bible, he doesn't read beyond the first few pages. The protagonist is fascinated by her mother's erudition: "I watched my autodidact mother swiftly, easily outstrip my father. The shelves in our lounge – which he built – filled up with second-hand books, Open University textbooks, political books, history books, books on race, books on gender, "All isms,'" as my father liked to call them. . ." (Smith 2016, 19). In the spirit of Virginia Woolf, the mother creates a room of her own, and a day of her own. Each Saturday, she takes a reprieve from parenting and wifehood and her husband and child are banished from morning until evening. Should they dare to return prematurely, they must contend with her ire.

Once the mother finishes her exams, she goes to college and then rises through the ranks and becomes a politician. She has made a path forward for herself and she expects the same for her daughter. To ensure that her daughter rises above her working-class status, she places her in a high-performing school. The mother regards her investment in her daughter's education as a mark of victory over the other women who are indifferent to her accomplishment. Their vision for the future rests on fantasy, the belief that their daughters' talent, the ability to dance and sing will provide a life beyond the council estate. As the novel reveals, talent is sparse and opportunities are few. While the narrator's best friend is able to earn a living as a dancer, her career is short-lived and she returns home and repeats the cycle of motherhood the narrator's mother wants her own daughter to avoid. Thus, Smith's statement is clear, education is the key to success, not just for daughters, but for mothers too. In a final act of independence, the mother moves out, leaving the daughter to be raised by her father. Taking this storyline further than in *On Beauty*, the mother enters into a lesbian relationship with her intellectual equal – free and liberated, truly a modern woman.

"I am the sole author of the dictionary that defines me" (Smith 2012, 3). These are the words of the protagonist of *NW*, and it is a mantra shared by Martha, Kiki and the mother in *Swing Time*, but some characters are quicker to reach this conclusion than others. Looking at the works together, it's clear Smith was slowly developing this radical black woman. From Martha's haphazard self-improvement plan to Kiki's slow evolution, by the time she reached *Swing Time*, Smith was committed to giving the black woman complete autonomy over her mind and body. She is the goddess Eruzulie personified, a bold, mythical figure captivating men and women alike. Ultimately, Smith creates a new literary model of black womanhood focused on intellectual transformative experiences that enable black women to be free and independent.

Works Cited

Arana, Victoria. "Intimations of William Blake in *On Beauty* (2005): Zadie Smith Trans-Atlantic Homage to and Critique of Boston Intellectuals." *Journal of Philosophy* 7, no. 17 (Spring): 2012. P.1 *Gale Academic OneFile*, link.gale.com/apps/doc/A284450874/AONE?u=sunysb&sid=AONE&xid=92f50589. Accessed 22 Jan. 2021.

Baumgartner, Kabria. *In Pursuit of Knowledge: Black Women and Educational Activism in Antebellum America*. New York: NYU Press. 2019.

Bazelon, Lara. "I've Picked My Job Over My Kids." *New York Times*, June 06, 2019. https://www.nytimes.com/2019/06/29/opinion/sunday/ive-picked-my-job-over-my-kids.html?searchResultPosition=1. Accessed October 5, 2020.

Billops, Camille. *Finding Christa*. Directed by Camille Billops and James Hatch. Criterion, 1991.

Collins, Patricia Hill. *Black Feminist Thought: Knowledge, Consciousness, and the Politics of Empowerment*. New York: Routledge. 2000.

Cooper, Anna Julia. *A Voice From the South*. Oxford: Oxford University Press. 1988.

Fischer, Susan. "'Gimme Shelter': Zadie Smith's On Beauty." In *Zadie Smith: Critical Essays*, Edited by Tracey Walters, New York: Peter Lang. 2008, 107–121.

Hurston, Neale Zora. *Their Eyes Were Watching God*. New York: Harper Perennial. 1990.

Lorde, Audre. *Sister Outsider*. Berkeley: Ten Speed Press. 2013.

Lourdes, Lopez-Ropero. "Searching for a 'Different Kind of freedom': Postcoloniality, Postfeminist Subjecthood in Zadie Smith's 'NW'." *Atlantis* (Salamanca Spain) vol. 38, no. 2, 2016, 123–139.

Marshall, Leni. "Through the Looking Glass: Revisiting Lacan and Woodward in Meconnaissance, the Mirror Stage of Old Age." *Feminist Formations*, vol. 24, no. 2 (Summer): 2012, 52–76. Project Muse.

Rich, Adrienne. *Of Woman Born: Motherhood as Experience and Institution*. New York: Bantam Books. 1977.

Smith, Zadie. *Martha and Hanwell*. London: Penguin Books. 2005a.

———. *On Beauty*. London: Hamish Hamilton. 2005b.

———. *Changing My Mind*. London: Penguin Books. 2009.

———. *NW*. 2012. London: Penguin Books, 2012.

———. *Swing Time*. London: Penguin Books, 2016.

———. "Motherhood is no Threat to Creativity." 12 June. *Telegraph.com*. 12 June 2013. https://www.telegraph.co.uk/culture/books/booknews/10116709/Motherhood-is-no-threat-to-creativity-author-Zadie-Smith-says.html. Accessed 17 December, 2020.

———. "The Bathroom." In *Feel Free: Essays*. London: Penguin Books. 2018, 354–364.

Walters, Tracey. "All Mammies and Hoes." In *Zadie Smith: Critical Essays*, Edited by Tracey Walters. New York: Peter Lang. 2008, 123–140.

Contributors

James Arnett is a UC Foundation Associate Professor of English at the University of Tennessee-Chattanooga, where he teaches twentieth- & twenty-first-century British and African literature. He is at work on a manuscript entitled *Un-bought and Unbiased: Conflict and Gender in 21st Century Zimbabwean Women's Literature*, as well as a book manuscript on Doris Lessing and the idea of significant otherness. He spent the academic year 2017–2018 on a Fulbright teaching/research fellowship in Bulawayo, Zimbabwe, and his articles have appeared in *PMLA*, *Callaloo*, *Genre*, *Ariel*, *African Literature Today*, and other journals.

Dr. Alberto Fernández Carbajal is Senior Lecturer in English Literature at the University of Roehampton (London, UK), where he teaches literature and creative writing. His research is placed at the intersection of colonial, postcolonial, queer, and diaspora studies, with a recent focus on Islam. He has published two monographs: *Compromise and Resistance in Postcolonial Writing: E. M. Forster's Legacy* (Palgrave Macmillan, 2014) and *Queer Muslim Diasporas in Contemporary Literature and Film* (Manchester University Press, 2019), the latter recently released in paperback. His new research project revolves around the notion of trans*versality, exploring how queer and trans Muslims depict themselves and are depicted by others across literature and the arts. He is the exiting Vice-Chair of the Postcolonial Studies Association (UK).

Daniel South holds a PhD in English Literature from the University of York. His research, funded by the Arts and Humanities Research Council, focussed on how contemporary novels operate in and provide models for the public sphere in the internet age. He is an Associate Fellow of the Higher Education Academy, and currently works for a widening participation charity in North London.

Matthias Stephan (Aarhus University, Denmark) researches postmodernism, and its implications in Gothic, sf, and crime fiction, as well as considerations of the transmodern, new materialism and ecocriticism. His work has appeared in *Scandinavian Studies*, *Coolabah* and the edited collections *Netflix Nostalgia and Transcending the Postmodern*, the latter with a transmodern consideration of Chimamanda Ngozi Adichie and Zadie Smith. His monograph *Defining Literary Postmodernism for the Twenty-First Century* is available at Palgrave. He is general editor for *Otherness: Essays and Studies*, and coordinator of the Centre for Studies in Otherness.

Tracey L. Walters is Professor of Literature in the Department of Africana Studies at Stony Brook University where she also holds an affiliate appointment with the Department of English, and Women's and Gender Studies. She is an interdisciplinary, transcultural scholar of Africana Studies, and writes about the experiences of African diasporic women through the lens of feminist studies and cultural studies. She is a leading scholar of Black British literature and *Classica Africana*, a subfield of classical studies. Her articles can be found in numerous journals and anthologies. She has published two monographs: *African American Women and the Classicists Tradition: Black Women Writers from Wheatley to Morrison* (Palgrave, 2007) and *Not Your Mother's Mammy: The Representation of the Domestic in Transatlantic Media* (Rutgers Press, 2021), and a reader *Today's Writers and their Works: Zadie Smith* (Cavendish Square Publishing, 2012). She also edited *Zadie Smith: Critical Essays* (Peter Lang, 2008) and was a guest editor for *Open Cultural Studies Journal*. She is the co-host of the podcast *Black Girls with Accents*.

www.ingramcontent.com/pod-product-compliance
Lightning Source LLC
Chambersburg PA
CBHW070912100726
47907CB00008B/2288

* 9 7 8 1 4 3 3 1 6 5 6 4 1 *